BUSINESS, TECHNOLOGY AND FINANCE

FINANCIAL PERFORMANCE

ANALYSIS, MEASURES AND IMPACT ON ECONOMIC GROWTH

BUSINESS, TECHNOLOGY AND FINANCE

Additional books in this series can be found on Nova's website
under the Series tab.

Additional e-books in this series can be found on Nova's website
under the e-book tab.

BUSINESS, TECHNOLOGY AND FINANCE

FINANCIAL PERFORMANCE

ANALYSIS, MEASURES AND IMPACT ON ECONOMIC GROWTH

ELAINE MORENO
EDITOR

nova publishers
New York

Library of Congress Cataloging-in-Publication Data

ISBN: 978-1-63484-501-4

Published by Nova Science Publishers, Inc. † New York

CONTENTS

PREFACE

Globally, family businesses constitute one of the pillars of social welfare, exerting an active and fundamental role in modern economies by generating wealth and creating jobs. This institution provides security and progress for family participants in the project, and benefits both the community and the national and international economic structure. To analyze its impact on the economy, Chapter One empirically examines the effect of the value generated by family business on economic growth worldwide, nationally and in industry sectors. Chapter Two studies whether the one-rule-fits-all approach adopted by the Nigerian Securities Exchange Commission promotes firm performance irrespective of the firms' ownership structures in Nigerian family owned firms. Chapter Three takes a close look at how corporate governance practices are evaluated by stock market participants. In Chapter Four, the link between financial inclusion, development and economic growth in low income countries is examined.

Chapter 1 - Globally, family business constitutes one of the pillars of social welfare, exerting an active and fundamental role in modern economies by generating wealth and creating jobs. This institution provides security and progress for family participants in the project, and benefits both the community and the national and international economic structure. To analyse its impact on the economy, this chapter empirically examines the effect of the value generated by family business on economic growth worldwide, nationally and in industry sectors. This analysis is based on a sample composed of the 17 largest companies in each of nine countries (Canada, France, Germany, Italy, Japan, Hong Kong, Spain, UK and USA), for the period 2002-2010. Using a panel data methodology, the authors analyse the role played by these companies in the economic growth of their countries of origin. The scope of this analysis is global, national and by activity sector. The authors' findings provide evidence of the positive influence on economic growth of the added value generated in each country by these companies, and concretely, the greater influence of the wealth generated by family firms. The influence of family firms is particularly significant in Italy and in the "basic materials" activity sector. The results obtained enhance the authors' understanding of the importance of these companies to the quality of life enjoyed in their countries of origin, and will enable policy makers to design strategies and actions to promote and facilitate the development of these firms.

Chapter 2 - *Manuscript type:* Empirical. *Purpose:* The purpose of this study is to empirically determine whether the one-rule-fits-all approached adopted by the Nigerian Securities Exchange Commission in terms of the separation of board chairman form the CEO promotes firm performance irrespective of the firms' ownership structures, in Nigerian with strong dominance of family owned firms.

Design/methodology/approach: The study is restricted to firms quoted on the Nigerian Stock Exchange. Pooled data for 18-years period 1994-2011 were collated from published annual reports and statement of accounts of 91 ownership dispersed firms and 72 ownership concentrated firms. Two equation system Ordinary Least Square multiple regressions were used to estimate the relationship between firm financial performance and CEO duality along ownership structures in Nigeria.

Findings: The findings of the study showed that while board duality was negative in predicting the financial performance of ownership dispersed firms; same cannot be said of ownership concentrated firms (family owned firms) as duality was found to be positive in predicting financial performance.

Research Limitations/Implications: Paucity of substantial local literature on institutional perspective of agency constitutes the major limitation of this study. Although, this study is meant to close this gap, the implication is that foreign theoretical and empirical literature standpoint constitutes the bulk of the review, which may not explain reasons for any identifiable local trends in Nigeria.

Practical Implication: The study reveals the importance of taking into cognizance, institutional perspective of agency theory in solving the excess power assigned to the board of directors, especially for family owned firms, where the family members have strong incentive to monitor the managers.

Originality/Value: This study contributes to the institutional perspective of agency theory from Nigerian institutional perspective. The study revealed the importance of accommodating individual country specificities in draft corporate governance laws.

Chapter 3 - This study takes a closer look at how corporate governance practices are evaluated by stock market participants. The recent study of Bebchuck, Cohen, and Wang (2013) has documented the disappearance of the governance-return association that existed during the 1990s. According to these authors, market participants have learned to fully appreciate corporate governance scores. This paper revisits this question by specifically looking at the association between revisions in corporate governance (CG) scores and subsequent stock returns. The authors therefore focus on the improvement or deterioration of CG quality, rather than its absolute value, as a potential source of stock market anomaly. The authors use an event study methodology to measure the market reaction to changes in the CG scores of 600 European public companies between 1999 and 2009. The results show that firms experiencing downward revisions are associated with long-term underperformance and weak and stable tracking-error volatility. This suggests that CG negative revisions is a source of abnormal returns that could be harnessed by professional financial analysts.

Chapter 4 - This study examines the link between financial inclusion, development and economic growth in low income countries (LICs). The analysis is quantitative, covering the period 1998-2013 and uses International Financial Statistics (IFS) and Bankscope data from the World Bank database. The use of a quantile regressions model in the analysis provides an extra level of robustness from earlier work and illuminates some interesting issues regarding the impact of financial inclusion. Depth of financial inclusion is significant in relation to economic growth compared with financial market depth. The study provides a strong case that the potential growth effect of financial institutions (banks) in LICs is much stronger relative to that of the financial market. Within the LIC context, the growth-enhancing effect of the financial sector thrives on the synergy of the financial institutions as it engenders wider inclusion. A significant outcome of this work is an increased appreciation of the importance of thorough analysis and the many cross dependencies. For policy makers there is a clear signal; don't develop plans around stimulating or reducing just one instrument in the economy and expect non-confounding results. The light shed on these key relationships suggest that policies on growth, financial sector reforms and financial inclusion need not be implemented in isolation. This is especially the case in LICs where institutional bottlenecks and structural constraints often widen the existing exclusion gap.

In: Financial Performance
Editor: Elaine Moreno

ISBN: 978-1-63484-501-4

Chapter 1

FAMILY BUSINESS AND ECONOMIC GROWTH: AN INTERNATIONAL ANALYSIS

***Isabel Mª García-Sánchez*[1], *Lázaro Rodríguez-Ariza*[2], *Jennifer Martínez-Ferrero*[1] *and José Daniel Lorenzo-Gómez*[3]**

[1]University of Salamanca, Salamanca, Spain
[2]University of Granada, Granada, Spain
[3]University of Cádiz, Cádiz, Spain

ABSTRACT

Globally, family business constitutes one of the pillars of social welfare, exerting an active and fundamental role in modern economies by generating wealth and creating jobs. This institution provides security and progress for family participants in the project, and benefits both the community and the national and international economic structure. To analyse its impact on the economy, this chapter empirically examines the effect of the value generated by family business on economic growth worldwide, nationally and in industry sectors. This analysis is based on a sample composed of the 17 largest companies in each of nine countries (Canada, France, Germany, Italy, Japan, Hong Kong, Spain, UK and USA), for the period 2002-2010. Using a panel data methodology, we analyse the role played by these companies in the economic growth of their countries of origin. The scope of this analysis is global, national and by activity sector. Our findings provide evidence of the positive influence on economic growth of the added value generated in each country by these companies, and concretely, the greater influence of the wealth generated by family firms. The influence of family firms is particularly significant in Italy and in the "basic materials" activity sector. The results obtained enhance our understanding of the importance of these companies to the quality of life enjoyed in their countries of origin, and will enable policy makers to design strategies and actions to promote and facilitate the development of these firms.

1. Introduction

One of the key aspects that have motivated researchers to analyse family firms is their impact on the economy and on the business community. In the European Union, 17 million firms are family firms (60% of the total), generating more than 100 million jobs. Furthermore, as a result of their dynamic growth and expansion, 25% of the top 100 companies in Europe are family controlled. In the United States, their importance is even greater: 90% of business organisations are family firms and they generate about 50% of total employment. These data highlight the outstanding importance of family firms in the economic sphere. In this regard, the data provided by various studies and organisations illustrate the vital significance of these firms, not only in terms of the number of companies, but also concerning the size of the workforce, the degree of internationalisation, the percentage of GDP they represent and relationships with the public sector (Chrisman et al., 2003).

Although these companies present many similarities with non-family firms (Sharma, 2004), they have other, unique characteristics that justify focusing research attention on this type of organisation. For example, Gómez-Mejía et al., (2001) and Berrone et al., (2010), among others, note the fundamental role played by family firms in the creation of human capital, commitment and firm-specific knowledge, as well as their greater ability to develop entrepreneurial behaviour patterns to ensure their survival (Zhara et al., 2004). These aspects, at least in part, determine their influence on the added value that is generated within the country (Moreno and Casillas, 2008), and more specifically, their influence on economic growth, in terms of gross domestic product (GDP).

The question of economic growth is one of the major concerns of our time, together with the search for a development strategy capable of overcoming the effects of the present economic and financial crisis, while promoting the growth of GDP.

For this reason, and taking as a starting point the points made above about the influence of family firms on the economy, in this chapter we analyse the added value generated by these businesses, as a determinant of economic growth. This added value is considered to be a crucial factor in any analysis of economic growth, in view of its positive effect on economic activity and growth.

In order to analyse this relationship, we examined a database composed of the 17 largest firms in each of nine countries (Canada, France, Germany, Italy, Japan, Hong Kong, Spain, UK and USA) for the period 2002-2010. The econometric analysis was performed using panel data techniques with fixed effects, splitting the study group into two samples, family and non-family firms, to analyse the contribution of each one. The findings provide descriptive and empirical evidence of the positive relationship between the added value generated by the largest companies and economic growth, and of the greater contribution made to growth when this added value is generated by family firms. Thus, the family business and, more specifically, the added value it generates in the country of origin, is a determinant of economic growth. This contribution to the economy by family firms is particularly significant in Italy and with respect to the "Basic materials" industry.

The rest of the chapter is structured as follows. Section two summarises the main theoretical issues concerning the family firm and its impact on economic growth, in order to propose the research hypothesis. The third section presents the model and the analysis technique applied, together with the data and samples used. The fourth section presents and discusses the results obtained; finally, the fifth section summarises the main conclusions drawn from this study.

2. Theoretical Framework: The Family Business and Economic Growth

The family firm constitutes one of the main strategic areas for the whole economy (Esparza-Aguilar et al., 2009) and is a major driver of activity, worldwide. For example, in the UK family firms represent about 75% of companies, and in the USA, 90%, contributing 60% of GDP and creating over 50 million jobs. Given the importance of the family firm in the economic sphere, this paper examines the effect made by the added value generated by family firms, as a determinant of economic development, taking into account that this business structure accounts for 75% of all companies worldwide (Nicholson, 2008). Nonetheless, before developing the study hypothesis, it is necessary to briefly discuss the concept of family firm, in order to conceptualise the field of study.

A clear and precise definition and conceptualisation of the family firm is needed, to clarify the dimensions of the question (Astrachan et al., 2002). In this regard, Chua et al., (1999) defined the essence of the family firm as follows: "*a business governed and/or managed with the intention to shape and pursue the vision of the business held by a dominant coalition controlled by members of the same family or a small number of families in a manner that is potentially sustainable across generations of the family or families*". Family firms usually present similar patterns of behaviour (Kashmiri and Mahajan, 2010), and maintain their fundamental positions within the management and the board (Arshad and Razak, 2011). For Basu (2000), the main features of family businesses are the long-term orientation of the family owners, their aim to retain family control of the company, their active participation in company management, in the definition of strategies and in the board, and the existence of inter-generational transfer.

The theory of resources and capacities has been adapted to the particular case of the family firm (Chrisman et al., 2003; Sharma, 2004), thus justifying its existence, its goal to obtain economic benefit and create value, and the competitive advantage it often enjoys[1]. This theory should be carefully considered in order to understand the competitive advantages that can be generated in the family business. Indeed, the involvement of the family within the company has led several authors (Habbershon and Williams, 1999; Sirmon and Hitt, 2003) to use the term "*familiness*" to refer to the distinguishing feature of the internal resources of the family firm, which allows it to maintain a strong competitive advantage, in terms of human and social capital, survival capital and corporate governance structure, among other aspects.

The competitive advantage of the family firm is the aspect that determines, at least in part, the added value generated by this type of firm (Lyagoubi, 2006). Thus, many studies have shown that more added value is generated by family than by non-family firms, primarily because family members take part in determining the strategy of the company, and do so on the basis of loyalty, flexibility and a long-term orientation (Shleifer and Vishny, 1997; Anderson and Reeb, 2003). In this respect, Kim (2006)

[1] According to Peteraf and Barney (2003), a company enjoys a competitive advantage whenever it is able to create greater marginal economic value than its competitors.

highlighted the existence of a positive relationship between family ownership and productivity, which produces a convergence of interest between controlling (family) shareholders and other shareholders, and noted that family shareholders influence financial and strategic decisions that impact on operations, debt and, consequently, on the value of the company (Lyagoubi, 2006). Martikainen et al., (2009) examined the firms in the S&P 500 list and found that family firms were more productive than comparable non-family firms, due to their more efficient use of labour and capital resources.

Nevertheless, little is known about the relationship between the added value generated, productivity and economic growth, in the context of family firms, although numerous studies have sought to analyse the determinants of economic growth, with many of them focusing on geographic, socio-demographic, cultural or macroeconomic variables[2]. The aim of the present study is to identify the types of ownership structure that exert most influence on economic development worldwide, addressing the relationship between economic growth and the added value generated by the family firm.

Curasi et al., (2004) offer one explanation for the positive influence of the family firm in economic development, claiming that family owners are more motivated to preserve and increase the wealth generated for future generations, and that this wealth directly influences the economic development of the country. To justify this association, however, we must take into account another distinguishing aspect of family firms, namely the professionalisation of their managers. This feature is evidenced in their greater capacity for innovation and in the better development of human resources and management policies within the family firm (Duréndez et al., 2007). Moreover, the family firm is characterised by a greater capacity for entrepreneurship and economic development, which allows it to discover new opportunities in periods of growth (Eddleston and Kellermanns, 2007; Bueno et al., 2013).

Although the literature on the subject is sparse, the family firm is known to be one of the drivers of greater social efficiency. It is the predominant form of company organisation and actively contributes to GDP and job creation in each country. For all these reasons, we hypothesise, therefore, that economic growth is determined by the greater added value generated by family

[2] For example, Crespo-Cuaresma et al. (2014) showed that human capital positively impacts on economic growth; in this respect, too, Moral-Benito (2012), employing Bayesian averaging of maximum likelihood estimates in panel data, identified the following robust determinants of economic growth: demographic factors, geographic factors, measures of openness and civil liberties, and macroeconomic indicators such as investment share. Finally, Hassan et al. (2011) highlighted the existence of a positive relationship between financial development and economic growth in developing countries.

businesses, and formulate this hypothesis as follows: "*The added value generated by the largest companies in each country has a positive impact on economic growth and is particularly significant among family firms*".

3. METHOD

3.1. Sample

The sample used to test our hypothesis comprised the largest international non-financial listed companies in each of nine countries – Canada, France, Germany, Italy, Japan, Hong Kong, Spain, UK and USA – for the period 2002–2010, a period during which a financial and economic crisis affected many countries. Following the criteria of La Porta et al., (2002), financial firms were excluded from the sample, due to the different characteristics of their equity, and because they are not comparable to non-financial firms. Taking into account data availability, our final sample was composed of the 17 largest companies in each of these nine countries, comprising a total of 153 companies. The sample is balanced and was obtained from information available in two databases: Thomson One Analytic for economic, financial and ownership data; and the World Bank's World Development Indicators 2014 (WDI) for the period 2002 to 2010.

3.2. Data

The aim of this chapter is to highlight the added value generated by family firms as a determinant of economic growth worldwide. In our analysis, the dependent variable is the economic growth of each country during the period 2002-2010 (Durlauf et al., 2005; Ciccone and Jarocinski, 2010; Madura and Ronquillo, 2008; Hassan et al., 2011; Moral-Benito, 2012; Crespo-Cuaresma et al., 2014). In this study, GDP growth rates are used as a proxy for economic growth. Thus, GDP is a numerical variable that represents the annual percentage growth rate of GDP at market prices based on constant local currency. GDP is the sum of the gross value added by all resident producers in the economy plus any product taxes and minus any subsidies not included in the value of the products. It is calculated without making deductions for depreciation of fabricated assets or for depletion and degradation of natural resources.

The main explanatory variable is the added value generated by the largest companies in each country. In this regard, Value_Added is a numerical variable that represents the net output of a sector after adding all outputs and subtracting intermediate inputs (Barth et al., 2005; Sánchez, 2013). It is calculated without making deductions for depreciation of fabricated assets or depletion and degradation of natural resources. This added value was determined by reference to the International Standard Industrial Classification (ISIC).

The main contribution of this study is the analysis performed of the contribution of family firms to economic growth. Several definitions of family firms have been proposed elsewhere, as have various operationalisations of these definitions (Uhlaner, 2005). However, most definitions coincide in that family firms are characterised by large investments in their capital and, frequently, by executive representation (Maury, 2006). In the present study, Family_Firm is a dummy variable that takes the value 1 when a company is considered to be a family firm and, 0 otherwise. We consider family firms to be those where one or more members of the founding family possess at least 25% of the ownership. This is one of the criteria that is most commonly adopted to identify family firms (De Massis et al., 2012; Campopiano et al., 2014).

In the literature on economic growth, the main area of interest is often the selection of appropriate variables to include in a linear regression to explain this growth, and in this respect over 140 variables have been identified (Hassan et al., 2011; Moral-Benito, 2012; Crespo-Cuaresma et al., 2014). To avoid biased results in our model, we incorporated a number of control variables, whose influence on economic growth has been tested previously: Population, Market_Cap, Industry_GDP, R&D_GDP and Trade_GDP. Population is a numerical variable that is based on the de facto definition of population, which counts all residents regardless of legal status or citizenship, except for refugees who are not permanently settled in the country of asylum, and who are generally considered to form part of the population of their country of origin. The values shown are midyear estimates; Market_Cap is a numerical variable that represents the share price multiplied by the number of shares outstanding. Listed domestic companies are the domestically incorporated companies listed on the country's stock exchanges at the end of the year. Listed companies do not include investment companies, mutual funds, or other collective investment vehicles. Data are in current U.S. dollars; Industry_GDP is a numerical variable that corresponds to ISIC divisions 10-45 and includes manufacturing (ISIC divisions 15-37). It comprises the value added in mining, manufacturing (also reported as a separate subgroup), construction, electricity, water and gas; R&D_GDP is a numerical variable that represents expenditure on research and development, defined as current and capital expenditure (both public and private) on creative work undertaken systematically to increase knowledge, including knowledge of humanity, culture and society, and the use of knowledge for new applications. R&D covers basic research, applied research and experimental development. Trade_GDP is a numerical variable that represents the sum of exports and imports of goods and services, measured as a share of gross domestic product. Additionally, we controlled for industry and year effects, and so $Industry_k$ are k dummy variables that represent the different k activity sectors in which the companies of the sample operate – i.e., energy, basic materials, industrial, construction, transportation and others; and $Year_t$ are t dummy variables that represent the t years of the sample, from 2002 to 2010.

3.3. Regression Specification

To test the hypothesis, several time series regressions for panel data are proposed. The basic model of analysis seeks to explain the GDP growth rate of an economy (ΔGDP) in terms of the added value generated by the largest companies in each country (Value_Added), with several control variables being incorporated in order to prevent the appearance of biased results.

The following relation is proposed to test our hypothesis:

$$\Delta GDP = f\,(\text{Value\_Added, Control variables})$$

This relation was empirically tested using the following dependence model for panel data for the full sample:

$$\Delta GDP_{it} = \beta_0 + \beta_1 Value\_Added_{it} + \beta_2 Population_{it} + \beta_3 Market\_GDP_{it} + \beta_4 Industry\_GDP_{it} + \beta_5 R\&D\_GDP_{it} + \beta_6 Trade\_GDP_{it} + \sum_{k=7}^{12} \beta_k Industry_i + \sum_{t=13}^{21} \beta_t Year_t + \mu_{it} + \eta_i$$

(Full sample)

where *i* represents the country and *t* represents the time period, β are estimated parameters, η_i represents the unobservable heterogeneity, and μ_{it} represents the classical disturbance term.

Specifically, we wished to compare the added value generated by family firms and by non-family firms. Therefore, the sample was divided into two sub-samples, in accordance with the criterion detailed in the Family_Firm variable. Thus we had one subsample of non-family firms, and another of family firms. The above-described dependence model was estimated for both subsamples. Then, two additional dependence models were proposed:

$$\Delta GDP_{it} = \alpha_0 + \alpha_1 Value\_Added_{it} + \alpha_2 Population_{it} + \alpha_3 Market\_GDP_{it} + \alpha_4 Industry\_GDP_{it} + \alpha_5 R\&D\_GDP_{it} + \alpha_6 Trade\_GDP_{it} + \sum_{k=7}^{12} \alpha_k Industry_i + \sum_{t=13}^{21} \alpha_t Year_t + \mu_{it} + \eta_i$$

(Non-family firms sample)

$$\Delta GDP_{it} = \gamma_0 + \gamma_1 Value\_Added_{it} + \gamma_2 Population_{it} + \gamma_3 Market\_GDP_{it} + \gamma_4 Industry\_GDP_{it} + \gamma_5 R\&D\_GDP_{it} + \gamma_6 Trade\_GDP_{it} + \sum_{k=7}^{12} \gamma_k Industry_i + \sum_{t=13}^{21} \gamma_t Year_t + \mu_{it} + \eta_i$$

(Family firms sample)

where *i* represents the country and *t* represents the time period, and are estimated parameters, η_i represents the unobservable heterogeneity, and μ_{it} represents the classical disturbance term.

Regression models for the panel data were then estimated. According to Hsiao (2007), panel data models (i) provide a more accurate inference, because a larger number of observations are used, and thus there are more degrees of freedom and the efficiency of the model is enhanced; (ii) control for omitted variables (missing or unobservable); (iii) capture the unobservable heterogeneity among individual units or over time; (iv) derive more accurate predictions for individual outcomes.

By using panel data we can assess economic growth over time by analysing the observations from several consecutive years for the same sample countries. Moreover, considering the temporal dimension of the data, particularly in periods of great change, significantly enriches the study. In this regard, panel data enable us to control for variations in economic growth each year, thus providing the analysis with a certain degree of dynamism and achieving both greater consistency and better explanatory power. Panel data also allow us to obtain more information about the same parameter, which provides greater efficiency. The parameters and the standard errors were estimated consistently in the model in order to derive valid inferences. Previous research findings were consulted to identify estimators capable of dealing with different endogeneity problems. However, not even the most robust methods can deal with all endogeneity problems, given the inconsistency of the model. Indeed, Pindado and Requejo (2012) stated that panel data are adequate for model specification and testing but warned against making predictions, because in the estimation process, part of the error term (i.e., the unobservable heterogeneity) was eliminated. Similarly, Lee (2006) argued that the consistency of parameter estimators and the validity of the economic interpretations made as marginal effects depended on the correct functional form specification and on controlling for unobserved heterogeneity. Accordingly, we applied the Hausman specification test to determine whether the random or the fixed model was most appropriate to control for this heterogeneity in the model (as recommended by Lee, 2006).

4. Results

4.1. Univariate Analysis

The sample analysed consists of 1,373 observations from nine countries for the period 2002-2010. Table 1 shows the sample distribution of family firms by year, industry and country. Panel A shows that the highest percentages refer to 2004, when family firms represented about 97% of the total of observations. In relation to the distribution by industry sector (Panel B), family firms are the largest companies in the industry and transportation activity sectors. Finally, in relation to geographic diversity (Panel C), in Canada, Italy, Japan, Spain and UK, all of the observations corresponding to the largest firms in each country are family firms, which underlines their significance in the economic sphere.

Table 2 summarises the mean rate of economic growth recorded expressed in millions of Euros, by year, industry and country. Panel A shows that economic growth was highest in 2006 (mean value, 2.7788). Regarding industry sector (Panel B) and country (Panel C), transportation was the activity sector presenting the highest mean level of economic growth (1.4645), while Spain (2.0807) followed by Canada (1.9442) were the countries that achieved the highest growth rate of GDP for the period analysed.

Table 1. Sample distribution of family firms by year, industry and country

Panel A. Sample distribution by year					
	Non-family firm		*Family firm*		*Total*
	Freq.	*Percent*	*Freq.*	*Percent*	*Freq.*
2002	6	3.95%	146	96.05%	152
2003	5	3.27%	148	96.73%	153
2004	4	2.61%	149	97.39%	153
2005	5	3.27%	148	96.73%	153
2006	5	3.27%	148	96.73%	153
2007	6	3.92%	147	96.08%	153
2008	6	3.92%	147	96.08%	153
2009	6	3.97%	145	96.03%	151
2010	8	5.26%	144	94.74%	152
Panel B. Sample distribution by industry					
	Non-family firm		*Family firm*		*Total*
	Freq.	*Percent*	*Freq.*	*Percent*	*Freq.*
Energy	18	3.96%	436	96.04%	454
Basic Materials	32	12.26%	229	87.74%	261
Industrial	0	0%	302	100%	302
Transportation	0	0%	247	100%	247
Construction	1	1.09%	91	98.91%	92
Others	0	0%	17	100%	17
Panel C. Sample distribution by country					
	Non-family firm		*Family firm*		*Total*
	Freq.	*Percent*	*Freq.*	*Percent*	*Freq.*
Canada	0	0%	153	100%	153
France	9	5.88%	144	94.12	153
Germany	6	3.92%	147	96.08%	153
Hong Kong	27	17.76%	125	82.24%	152
Italy	0	0%	150	100%	150
Japan	0	0%	153	100%	153
Spain	0	0%	153	100%	153
UK	0	0%	153	100%	153
USA	9	5.88%	144	94.12%	153

Sample. 1,373 observations of 9 countries in 2002-2010.

Table 2. Economic growth by year, industry and country

Panel A. Year		
	Mean	*Sd. Dev.*
2002	1.4586	1.1216
2003	1.7843	1.5604
2004	2.5628	0.8063
2005	2.2039	1.1118
2006	2.7788	0.7841
2007	2.4063	0.7518
2008	0.0819	0.9051
2009	-4.0504	1.3327
2010	2.5374	1.3939
Panel B. Industry		
	Mean	*Sd. Dev.*
Energy	1.4156	2.3526
Basic Materials	1.3730	2.2324
Industrial	1.1109	2.3736
Transportation	1.4645	2.3374
Construction	1.2611	2.1261
Others	0.7841	3.0251
Panel C. Country		
	Mean	*Sd. Dev.*
Canada	1.9442	1.7830
France	1.1431	1.6479
Germany	0.8513	2.7975
Hong Kong	1.7309	2.2008
Italy	0.2458	2.1290
Japan	0.8452	2.6902
Spain	2.0807	2.3681
UK	1.6533	2.4101
USA	1.7371	1.9479

Sample. 1,373 observations of 9 countries in 2002-2010.

Table 3. Descriptive statistics and bivariate correlations

	Mean	Std. Dev.	1	2	3	4	5	6	7	8
ΔGDP	1.3138	2.3247	1							
Value_Added	141272.3	111273.6	0.0040	1						
Family_Firm	0.9628	0.1892	0.0138	0.0097	1					
Popula-tion	8.79e + 07	8.29e + 07	0.015	0.0841	0.0239	1				
Market_Cap	3.37e + 12	4.75e + 12	0.114	0.0801	-0.0152	0.0938	1			
Industry_GDP	25.5504	3.5129	0.1321	-0.4285	0.0978	-0.4116	0.4748	1		
R&D_GDP	1.9592	0.7809	-0.0964	0.4438	0.1026	0.0597	0.4285	-0.0472	1	
Trade_GDP	81.4981	101.438	0.0945	-0.4247	-0.2629	-0.4307	-0.2706	0.3548	-0.0576	1

Sample. 1,373 observations of 9 countries in 2002-2010.

Variables. ΔGDP is a numerical variable that represents the annual percentage growth rate of GDP at market prices based on constant local currency. GDP is the sum of the gross value added by all resident producers in the economy plus any product taxes and minus any subsidies not included in the value of the products. It is calculated without making deductions for depreciation of fabricated assets or for depletion and degradation of natural resources. Value_Added is a numerical variable that represents the net output of a sector after adding all outputs and subtracting intermediate inputs. It is calculated without making deductions for depreciation of fabricated assets or depletion and degradation of natural resources. The origin of value added is determined by the International Standard Industrial Classification (ISIC), revision 3; Family_Firm is a dummy variable that takes the value 1 when a company is considered a family firm and 0 otherwise. We consider family firms those where a member of the founding family has at least 25% of the ownership (De Massis et al., 2012; Campopiano et al., 2014); Population is a numerical variable that is based on the de facto definition of population, which counts all residents regardless of legal status or citizenship -except for refugees not permanently settled in the country of asylum, who are generally considered part of the population of their country of origin. The values shown are midyear estimates; Market_Cap is a numerical variable that represents the share price multiplied by the number of shares outstanding. (Continued).

Listed domestic companies are the domestically incorporated companies listed on the country's stock exchanges at the end of the year. Listed companies do not include investment companies, mutual funds, or other collective investment vehicles. Data are in current U.S. dollars; Industry_GDP is a numerical variable that corresponds to ISIC divisions 10-45 and includes manufacturing (ISIC divisions 15-37). It comprises value added in mining, manufacturing (also reported as a separate subgroup), construction, electricity, water, and gas; R&D_GDP is a numerical variable that represents the expenditure on research and development in current and capital expenditure (both public and private) on creative work undertaken systematically to increase knowledge, including knowledge of humanity, culture, and society, and the use of knowledge for new applications. R&D covers basic research, applied research, and experimental development; Trade_GDP is a numerical variable that represents the sum of exports and imports of goods and services measured as a share of gross domestic product.

Table 3 shows the mean values for the variables included in this analysis. Among these, there was a positive rate of economic growth, with a mean value of 1.3138% of growth. For Value_Added, a mean value of 141272.3 was recorded. The results for the Family_Firms variable show that this business structure represents around 96% of the sample. These findings corroborate the observation that in Europe over 60% of firms are family controlled, and in USA, the corresponding figure is about 90%. Table 3 also shows the bivariate correlations between the variables used in the model. In no case were high values obtained for the coefficients between dependent and independent variables or between the independent variables.

4.2. Multivariate Analysis

Our main aim in this chapter is to analyse the association between the added value generated by the largest firms in each country and the economic growth recorded in each case. More specifically, we hypothesise that this association is stronger if the added value is generated by family firms.

Several statistical assumptions were used to analyse the regressions proposed. The likelihood of multicollinearity and heteroskedasticity problems and of common method bias were analysed for the full sample and for each subsample (family firms and non-family firms). With regard to normality, application of the Kolmogorov-Smirnov test showed that the variables do not present a normal distribution. Nevertheless, according to Green (1999), the assumption of normality may be considered unnecessary to obtain most of the results normally reported in multiple regression analysis.

With respect to the existence of unobservable heterogeneity between countries, two different cases are noted: on the one hand, when heterogeneity is correlated with the explanatory variables (fixed effects), and on the other, when it is independent of them (random effects). The choice between the two models was made after an analysis of the Hausman test. This test verifies the null hypothesis of the absence of correlation between the individual effects and the independent variables, and the possibility that there is no systematic difference between random effects and fixed effects (Prob > chi2 > 0.00). When this is rejected, the higher degree of efficiency in the estimation leads us to use the fixed-effects model. For all of the proposed models, the Hausman null hypothesis was rejected, and therefore the fixed-effects model was considered more appropriate to obtain more efficient coefficients.

With regard to the explanatory power of the model (R^2), Green (1999) considered an R^2 of 0.50 to be relatively high, although whether a regression gives a good fit to the model depends on the framework. In all of the proposed models, the highest R^2 values obtained were above 0.50, and most of them were about 0.90. Therefore, these values did not exclude the viability of the models in question, whose explanatory capability was corroborated.

Table 4 summarises the results obtained for the dependency models. As mentioned above, the full sample was divided into two subsamples in order to analyse the influence of the added value generated by family and non-family firms on the overall rate of economic growth. The empirical findings are presented by reference to the three models specified (full sample, non-family firms and family-firms). The first column in Table 4 shows that the added value generated by the largest firms in each country has a positive impact on economic growth (coef. 7.27e-06, significant at 99% confidence level). Moreover, the positive effect on economic growth of this added value is especially apparent in the family firms subsample. This is reflected in the Value_Added coefficient of 7.09E-06, which is significant at a 99% confidence level, while for the non-family firms′ sample, the main explanatory variable is not statistically significant. These results corroborate our hypothesis regarding the influence made by family firms on the added value generated nationally (Moreno and Casillas, 2008), and more specifically, the influence on economic growth, as represented by the rate of growth of GDP. Theoretical support for our findings is provided by Curasi et al., (2004), who assert that the owners of family firms show a greater motivation and concern to preserve and increase the wealth generated for future generations, thus increasing the overall rate of economic growth. Furthermore, our results are in line with those of Duréndez et al., (2007), Eddleston and Kellermanns (2007) and Bueno et al., (2013), who observed a positive relation between the family firm and economic growth, due to the greater capacity for innovation and entrepreneurship among these firms.

To complement the evidence obtained, a regression analysis was performed on the above model (for the three samples: full sample, non-family and family firms) by country and by industry sector. The aim of this analysis was to highlight the most significant effects, for each country and industry sector. Table 5 summarises the findings by country, and Table 6, the results by industry sector. For the per-country analysis, as in the initial overall analysis, the results highlighted the positive association between the value added and the economic growth achieved in each of the nine countries analysed; the Value_Added coefficient was positive and significant in every case.

Table 4. The impact on rates of economic growth of the value added by the largest companies

	Full Sample		Non-family firms		Family firms	
Dependent variable = ΔGDP	*Coef.*	*Std. Err.*	*Coef.*	*Std. Err.*	*Coef.*	*Std. Err.*
Value_Added	7.27e-06***	1.53e-06	0.0000177	0.0000128	7.09E-06***	1.55E-06
Population	-1.41e-07***	2.69e-08	-1.56E-07	1.74E-07	-1.46E-07***	2.77E-08
Market_Cap	2.58e-13***	4.67e-14	-6.94E-14	3.33E-13	2.65E-13***	4.77E-14
Industry_GDP	0.8529***	0.1002	2.65248**	1.397487	0.8449614***	0.1006364
R&D_GDP	-9.9943***	0.7073	-13.03983	8.198637	-9.952259***	0.7123589
Trade_GDP	0.1491***	0.0222	-0.2324048	0.3018293	0.150453***	0.0223219
_cons	-319.393***	111.2935	-2196.729	1606.5	-312.4739***	111.8625
Industry	*Controlled*		*Controlled*		*Controlled*	
Year	*Controlled*		*Controlled*		*Controlled*	
sigma_u	17.946		18.1234		18.2920	
sigma_e	1.621		1.8056		1.6214	
Rho	0.992		0.9902		0.9922	
R^2	0.5451		0.9945		0.5451	
Hausman test (Prob>chi2)	0.000		0.000		0.000	

Sample: 1,373 observations of 9 countries in 2002-2012.

Variables: ΔGDP is a numerical variable that represents the annual percentage growth rate of GDP at market prices based on constant local currency. GDP is the sum of the gross value added by all resident producers in the economy plus any product taxes and minus any subsidies not included in the value of the products. It is calculated without making deductions for depreciation of fabricated assets or for depletion and degradation of natural resources. Value_Added is a numerical variable that represents the net output of a sector after adding all outputs and subtracting intermediate inputs. It is calculated without making deductions for depreciation of fabricated assets or depletion and degradation of natural resources. The origin of value added is determined by the International Standard Industrial Classification (ISIC), revision 3; Family_Firm is a dummy variable that takes the value 1 when a company is considered a family firm and 0 otherwise. (Continued).

We consider family firms those where a member of the founding family has at least 25% of the ownership (De Massis et al., 2012; Campopiano et al., 2014); Population is a numerical variable that is based on the de facto definition of population, which counts all residents regardless of legal status or citizenship -except for refugees not permanently settled in the country of asylum, who are generally considered part of the population of their country of origin. The values shown are midyear estimates; Market_Cap is a numerical variable that represents the share price times the number of shares outstanding. Listed domestic companies are the domestically incorporated companies listed on the country's stock exchanges at the end of the year. Listed companies do not include investment companies, mutual funds, or other collective investment vehicles. Data are in current U.S. dollars; Industry_GDP is a numerical variable that corresponds to ISIC divisions 10-45 and includes manufacturing (ISIC divisions 15-37). It comprises value added in mining, manufacturing (also reported as a separate subgroup), construction, electricity, water, and gas; R&D_GDP is a numerical variable that represents the expenditure on research and development in current and capital expenditure (both public and private) on creative work undertaken systematically to increase knowledge, including knowledge of humanity, culture, and society, and the use of knowledge for new applications. R&D covers basic research, applied research, and experimental development; Trade_GDP is a numerical variable that represents the sum of exports and imports of goods and services measured as a share of gross domestic product; $Industry_k$ are k dummy variables that represent the different k activity sectors in which the companies of the sample operate – i.e., energy, basic materials, industrial, construction, transportation and others; and $Year_t$ are t dummy variables that represent the t years of the sample, from 2002 to 2010. *, **, and *** represent statistical significance at 95%, 99% and 99.9%, respectively.

Table 5. The impact on rates of economic growth, by country, of the value added by the largest companies

Canada					
	Full Sample		Non-family firms	Family firms	
Dependent variable = ΔGDP	*Coef.*	*Std. Err.*	*No observations*	*Coef.*	*Std. Err.*
Value_Added	0.0002*	0.361266		0.0002*	0.361266
Population	-5.11E-06*	0.001258		-5.11E-06*	0.001258
Market_Cap	7.16E-13	1.85Ee12		7.16E-13	1.85Ee12
Industry_GDP	0.62531	1.851236		0.62531	1.851236
R&D_GDP	0.18125**	23.36256		0.18125**	23.36256
Trade_GDP	0.1495*	0.253612		0.1495*	0.253612
_cons	210.2152***	23.65823		210.2152***	23.65823
Industry	*Controlled*			*Controlled*	
Year	*Controlled*			*Controlled*	
sigma_u	15.236232			15.236232	
sigma_e	1.5236121			1.5236121	
Rho	0.9933520			0.9933520	
R^2	0.9978			0.9978	
Hausman test (Prob>chi2)	0.001			0.001	
France					
	Full Sample		Non-family firms	Family firms	
Dependent variable = ΔGDP	*Coef.*	*Std. Err.*	*Insufficient observations*	*Coef.*	*Std. Err.*
Value_Added	0.000244***	8.23E-06		0.000244***	8.23E-06
Population	0.00045***	2.34E-06		0.00045***	2.34E-06
Market_Cap	3.02E-13***	8.91E-14		3.02E-13***	8.91E-14
Industry_GDP	-10.16894***	0.378220		-10.16894***	0.378220
R&D_GDP	45.89254***	2.5228		45.89254***	2.5228
Trade_GDP	-60.23948***	0.04138		-60.23948***	0.04138
_cons	41552.81***	1920.689		41552.81***	1920.689
Industry	*Controlled*			*Controlled*	
Year	*Controlled*			*Controlled*	
sigma_u	0.0522			0.0522	
sigma_e	0.2597			0.2597	
Rho	0.0388			0.0388	
R^2	0.9757			0.9757	
Hausman test (Prob>chi2)	0.000			0.000	

Table 5. (Continued).

Germany					
	Full Sample		Non-family firms	Family firms	
Dependent variable = ΔGDP	*Coef.*	*Std. Err.*	*Insufficient observations*	*Coef.*	*Std. Err.*
Value_Added	0.00007***	1.99E-07		0.00007***	1.99E-07
Population	-1.33E-06***	4.79E-08		-1.33E-06***	4.79E-08
Market_Cap	2.59E-12***	1.39E-14		2.59E-12***	1.39E-14
Industry_GDP	4.6677***	0.006219		4.6677***	0.006219
R&D_GDP	-20.2638***	0.101068		-20.2638***	0.101068
Trade_GDP	-0.44671***	0.001352		-0.44671***	0.001352
_cons	-2630.509***	16.02583		-2630.509***	16.02583
Industry	*Controlled*			*Controlled*	
Year	*Controlled*			*Controlled*	
sigma_u	0.00257			0.00257	
sigma_e	0.02107			0.02107	
Rho	0.01472			0.01472	
R^2	0.9987			0.9987	
Hausman test (Prob>chi2)	0.001			0.001	
Hong-Kong					
	Full Sample		Non-family firms	Family firms	
Dependent variable =	*Coef.*	*Std. Err.*	*Insufficient observations*	*Coef.*	*Std. Err.*
Value_Added	0.0002486***	1.43e-05		0.0002486***	1.43e-05
Population	0.000024***	1.29e-08		0.000024***	1.29e-08
Market_Cap	3.25E-12***	2.67e-14		3.25E-12***	2.67e-14
Industry_GDP	-3.25431***	0.32102		-3.25431***	0.32102
R&D_GDP	21.24541***	0.13553		21.24541***	0.13553
Trade_GDP	1.154356***	0.2563		1.154356***	0.2563
_cons	623.25***	79.5812		623.25***	79.5812
Industry	*Controlled*			*Controlled*	
Year	*Controlled*			*Controlled*	
sigma_u	0.001251			0.001251	
sigma_e	0.01522			0.01522	
Rho	0.00785			0.00785	
R^2	0.9553			0.9553	
Hausman test (Prob>chi2)	0.000			0.000	

Italy					
	Full Sample		Non-family firms	Family firms	
Dependent variable = ΔGDP	*Coef.*	*Std. Err.*	*No observations*	*Coef.*	*Std. Err.*
Value_Added	0.00124***	0.00002		0.00124***	0.00002
Population	0.000012***	2.79E-06		0.000012***	2.79E-06
Market_Cap	6.51E-12***	8.31E-13		6.51E-12***	8.31E-13
Industry_GDP	-6.53960***	0.629832		-6.53960***	0.629832
R&D_GDP	23.57799***	5.886039		23.57799***	5.886039
Trade_GDP	1.297967***	0.116551		1.297967***	0.116551
_cons	12420.43***	1945.652		12420.43***	1945.652
Industry	*Controlled*			*Controlled*	
Year	*Controlled*			*Controlled*	
sigma_u	0.01335			0.01335	
sigma_e	0.58749			0.58749	
Rho	0.00051			0.00051	
R^2	0.9347			0.9347	
Hausman test (Prob > chi2)	0.000			0.000	
Japan					
	Full Sample		Non-family firms	Family firms	
Dependent variable = ΔGDP	*Coef.*	*Std. Err.*	*No observations*	*Coef.*	*Std. Err.*
Value_Added	8.96E-06***	7.82E-07		-8.96E-06***	7.82E-07
Population	-4.40E-06***	3.47E-07		-4.40E-06***	3.47E-07
Market_Cap	6.06E-13***	2.30E-14		6.06E-13***	2.30E-14
Industry_GDP	5.86494***	0.079485		5.86494***	0.079485
R&D_GDP	-0.583811***	0.508858		-0.583811***	0.508858
Trade_GDP	-0.222607***	0.0173122		-0.222607***	0.0173122
_cons	-3083.007***	51.6701		-3083.007***	51.6701
Industry	*Controlled*			*Controlled*	
Year	*Controlled*			*Controlled*	
sigma_u	0.039556			0.039556	
sigma_e	0.14483			0.14483	
Rho	0.06941			0.06941	
R^2	0.9976			0.9976	
Hausman test (Prob>chi2)	0.000			0.000	

Table 5. (Continued).

Spain					
	Full Sample		Non-family firms	Family firms	
Dependent variable = ΔGDP	*Coef.*	*Std. Err.*	*No observations*	*Coef.*	*Std. Err.*
Value_Added	0.00015***	5.04E-06		-0.00015***	5.04E-06
Population	-5.77E-16***	1.52E-07		-5.77E-16***	1.52E-07
Market_Cap	1.64E-12***	4.41E-14		1.64E-12***	4.41E-14
Industry_GDP	2.8608***	0.05487		2.8608***	0.05487
R&D_GDP	21.9324***	1.18165		21.9324***	1.18165
Trade_GDP	0.58007***	0.00678		0.58007***	0.00678
_cons	-9976.578***	179.6241		-9976.578***	179.6241
Industry	*Controlled*			*Controlled*	
Year	*Controlled*			*Controlled*	
sigma_u	0.00054			0.00054	
sigma_e	0.11474			0.11474	
rho	0.00002			0.00002	
R^2	0.9979			0.9979	
Hausman test (Prob>chi2)	0.000			0.000	
UK					
	Full Sample		Non-family firms	Family firms	
Dependent variable = ΔGDP	*Coef.*	*Std. Err.*	*No observations*	*Coef.*	*Std. Err.*
Value_Added	0.000056***	9.01E-06			
Population	0.000016***	2.24E-06			
Market_Cap	-2.97E-13***	3.92E-13			
Industry_GDP	16.06583***	2.141864			
R&D_GDP	-70.58137***	4.66933			
Trade_GDP	-3.44108***	0.52341			
_cons	-9018.368***	4333.015			
Industry	*Controlled*			*Controlled*	
Year	*Controlled*			*Controlled*	
sigma_u	0.28336			0.28336	
sigma_e	0.85059			0.85059	
rho	0.09989			0.09989	
R^2	0.8583			0.8583	
Hausman test (Prob>chi2)	0.000			0.000	

USA					
	Full Sample		Non-family firms	Family firms	
Dependent variable = ΔGDP	*Coef.*	*Std. Err.*	*Insufficient observations*	*Coef.*	*Std. Err.*
Value_Added	2.35E-06***	8.13E-07		2.35E-06***	8.13E-07
Population	-5.42E-06***	3.35E-07		-5.42E-06***	3.35E-07
Market_Cap	5.73E-13***	3.26E-14		5.73E-13***	3.26E-14
Industry_GDP	-3.95882*	0.112247		-3.95882*	0.112247
R&D_GDP	-2.423591***	1.43369		-2.423591***	1.43369
Trade_GDP	1.56111***	0.041176		1.56111***	0.041176
_cons	-23875.06***	1681.085		-23875.06***	1681.085
Industry	*Controlled*			*Controlled*	
Year	*Controlled*			*Controlled*	
sigma_u	0.08540			0.08540	
sigma_e	0.21887			0.21887	
rho	0.0618			0.0618	
R^2	0.9886			0.9886	
Hausman test (Prob>chi2)	0.000			0.000	

Sample: 1,373 observations of 9 countries in 2002-2012.

Variables: ΔGDP is a numerical variable that represents the annual percentage growth rate of GDP at market prices based on constant local currency. GDP is the sum of the gross value added by all resident producers in the economy plus any product taxes and minus any subsidies not included in the value of the products. It is calculated without making deductions for depreciation of fabricated assets or for depletion and degradation of natural resources. Value_Added is a numerical variable that represents the net output of a sector after adding all outputs and subtracting intermediate inputs. It is calculated without making deductions for depreciation of fabricated assets or depletion and degradation of natural resources. The origin of value added is determined by the International Standard Industrial Classification (ISIC), revision 3; Family_Firm is a dummy variable that takes the value 1 when a company is considered a family firm and, 0 otherwise. We consider family firms those where a member of the founding family has at least 25% of the ownership (De Massis et al., 2012; Campopiano et al., 2014); Population is a numerical variable that is based on the de facto definition of population, which counts all residents regardless of legal status or citizenship -except for refugees not permanently settled in the country of asylum, who are generally considered part of the population of their country of origin. The values shown are midyear estimates; Market_Cap is a numerical variable that represents the share price times the number of shares outstanding. Listed domestic companies are the domestically incorporated companies listed on the country's stock exchanges at the end of the year. Listed companies do not include investment companies, mutual funds, or other collective investment vehicles. Data are in current U.S. dollars; Industry_GDP is a numerical variable that corresponds to ISIC divisions 10-45 and includes manufacturing (ISIC divisions 15-37). It comprises value added in mining, manufacturing (also reported as a separate subgroup), construction, electricity, water, and gas; R&D_GDP is a numerical variable that represents the expenditure on research and development in current and capital expenditure (both public and private) on creative work undertaken systematically to increase knowledge, including knowledge of humanity, culture, and society, and the use of knowledge for new applications. R&D covers basic research, applied research, and experimental development; Trade_GDP is a numerical variable that represents the sum of exports and imports of goods and services measured as a share of gross domestic product; $Industry_k$ are k dummy variables that represent the different k activity sectors in which the companies of the sample operate – i.e., energy, basic materials, industrial, construction, transportation and others; and $Year_t$ are t dummy variables that represent the t years of the sample, from 2002 to 2010.

*, **, and *** represent statistical significance at 95%, 99% and 99.9%, respectively.

Table 6. The impact on rates of economic growth, by industry, of the value added by the largest companies

Energy					
	Full Sample		Non-family firms	Family firms	
Dependent variable = ΔGDP	*Coef.*	*Std. Err.*	*Insufficient observations*	*Coef.*	*Std. Err.*
Value_ Added	6.34E-06**	2.82E-06		6.34E-06**	2.82E-06
Population	-1.21E-07**	6.42E-08		-1.21E-07**	6.42E-08
Market_ Cap	5.51E-13***	1.10E-13		5.51E-13***	1.10E-13
Industry_ GDP	0.8852702***	0.165052		0.8852702***	0.165052
R&D_GDP	-9.082564**	1.196334		-9.082564**	1.196334
Trade_ GDP	0.1496181***	0.036824		0.1496181***	0.036824
_cons	-349.1884	186.2091		-349.1884	186.2091
Year	*Controlled*			*Controlled*	
sigma_u	12.436835			12.436835	
sigma_e	1.6112118			1.6112118	
rho	0.98349343			0.98349343	
R^2	0.5750			0.5750	
Hausman test (Prob>chi2)	0.000			0.000	

Basic Materials						
	Full Sample		Non-family firms		Family firms	
Dependent variable = ΔGDP	*Coef.*	*Std. Err.*	*Coef.*	*Std. Err.*	*Coef.*	*Std. Err.*
Value_ Added	8.91E-06***	2.80E-06	0.0000177	0.0000128	8.44E-06***	2.90E-06
Population	-1.33E-07**	5.35E-08	-1.56E-07	1.74E-07	-1.54E-07**	5.90E-08
Market_ Cap	1.42E-13	9.21E-14	-6.94E-14	3.33E-13	1.55E-13	9.87E-14
Industry_ GDP	0.8696963***	0.2360175	2.65248**	1.397487	0.8120098***	0.2401112
R&D_ GDP	-11.01353***	1.779291	-13.03983	8.198637	-10.94939***	1.853801
Trade_ GDP	0.1166096**	0.0548318	-0.232408	0.3018293	0.1238328**	0.0561095
_cons	-280.0176	274.1137	-2195.915	1606.237	-222.5741	279.4655

	Full Sample		Non-family firms	Family firms	
Dependent variable = ΔGDP	*Coef.*	*Std. Err.*	*No observations*	*Coef.*	*Std. Err.*
Year	*Controlled*		*Controlled*	*Controlled*	
sigma_u	19.133122		18.320589	21.249211	
sigma_e	1.5603002		1.8055543	1.55073	
rho	0.99339358		0.99038068	0.99470239	
R^2	0.5327		0.6696	0.5331	
Hausman test (Prob>chi2)	0.002		0.000	0.002	
Industrial					
	Full Sample		Non-family firms	Family firms	
Dependent variable = ΔGDP	*Coef.*	*Std. Err.*	*No observations*	*Coef.*	*Std. Err.*
Value_ Added	6.14E-06*	3.10E-06		6.14E-06*	3.10E-06
Population	-1.18E-07**	4.75E-08		-1.18E-07**	4.75E-08
Market_Cap	1.51E-13**	8.09E-14		1.51E-13**	8.09E-14
Industry_ GDP	0.9184631***	0.2297967		0.9184631***	0.229796
R&D_GDP	-10.5945***	1.401629		-10.5945***	1.401629
Trade_GDP	0.1821733***	0.0446554		0.1821733***	0.0446554
_cons	-222.5743	224.2359		-222.5743	224.2359
Year	*Controlled*			*Controlled*	
sigma_u	18.437355			18.437355	
sigma_e	1.5893343			1.5893343	
rho	0.99262405			0.99262405	
R^2	0.5795			0.5795	
Hausman test (Prob>chi2)	0.000			0.000	
Transportation					
	Full Sample		Non-family firms	Family firms	
Dependent variable = ΔGDP	*Coef.*	*Std. Err.*	*Insufficient observations*	*Coef.*	*Std. Err.*
Value_Added	5.40E-06***	4.48E-06		5.40E-06***	4.48E-06
Population	-1.27E-0*7	7.43E-08		-1.27E-0*7	7.43E-08
Market_Cap	2.87E-13**	1.33E-13		2.87E-13**	1.33E-13
Industry_GDP	0.9937331***	0.2600733		0.993731***	0.2600733
R&D_GDP	-10.96603***	2.057881		-10.9660***	2.057881
Trade_GDP	0.1201306**	0.0593227		0.1201306**	0.0593227
_cons	-537.8458	303.8657		-537.8458	303.8657

Table 6. (Continued).

	Full Sample		Non-family firms	Family firms	
Dependent variable = ΔGDP	*Coef.*	*Std. Err.*	*Insufficient observations*	*Coef.*	*Std. Err.*
Year	*Controlled*			*Controlled*	
sigma_u	17.63786			17.63786	
sigma_e	1.721793			1.721793	
Rho	0.99056045			0.99056045	
R^2	0.5425			0.5425	
Hausman test (Prob>chi2)	0.001			0.001	
Construction					
	Full Sample		Non-family firms	Family firms	
Dependent variable	*Coef.*	*Std. Err.*	*Insufficient*	*Coef.*	*Std. Err.*
Value_ Added	6.75E-06	7.51E-06		6.75E-06	7.51E-06
Population	-1.47E-07	1.17E-07		-1.47E-07	1.17E-07
Market_Cap	2.47E-13	1.98E-13		2.47E-13	1.98E-13
Industry_ GDP	0.8527741	0.4231286		0.8527741	0.4231286
R&D_GDP	-11.74655**	2.950973		-11.74655**	2.950973
Trade_GDP	0.1244503***	0.1038463		0.124450***	0.1038463
_cons	-443.629	464.877		-443.629	464.877
Year	*Controlled*			*Controlled*	
sigma_u	18.412731			18.412731	
sigma_e	1.7074877			1.7074877	
Rho	0.99147371			0.99147371	
R^2	0.4780			0.4780	
Hausman test (Prob>chi2)	0.000			0.000	
Others					
	Full Sample		Non-family firms	Family firms	
Dependent variable = ΔGDP	*Coef.*	*Std. Err.*	*Insufficient observations*	*Coef.*	*Std. Err.*
Value_ Added	0.0002445	0.0001239		0.0002445	0.0001239
Population	9.59E-06	0.0000115		9.59E-06	0.0000115
Market_Cap	5.43E-12	1.97E-12		5.43E-12	1.97E-12
Industry_ GDP	4.984809	1.909422		4.984809	1.909422
R&D_GDP	-8.542665	48.04699		-8.542665	48.04699
Trade_GDP	-0.649392	0.361266		-0.649392	0.361266
_cons	-3819.668	2469.375		-3819.668	2469.375

	Full Sample		Non-family firms	Family firms	
Dependent variable = ΔGDP	*Coef.*	*Std. Err.*	*Insufficient observations*	*Coef.*	*Std. Err.*
Year	*Controlled*			*Controlled*	
sigma_u	199.44737			199.44737	
sigma_e	1.3420725			1.3420725	
Rho	0.99995472			0.99995472	
R^2	0.9779			0.9779	
Hausman test (Prob>chi2)	0.003			0.003	

Sample: 1,373 observations of 9 countries in 2002-2012.

Variables: ΔGDP is a numerical variable that represents the annual percentage growth rate of GDP at market prices based on constant local currency. GDP is the sum of the gross value added by all resident producers in the economy plus any product taxes and minus any subsidies not included in the value of the products. It is calculated without making deductions for depreciation of fabricated assets or for depletion and degradation of natural resources. Value_Added is a numerical variable that represents the net output of a sector after adding all outputs and subtracting intermediate inputs. It is calculated without making deductions for depreciation of fabricated assets or depletion and degradation of natural resources. The origin of value added is determined by the International Standard Industrial Classification (ISIC), revision 3; Family_Firm is a dummy variable that takes the value 1 when a company is considered a family firm and, 0 otherwise. We consider family firms those where a member of the founding family has at least 25% of the ownership (De Massis et al., 2012; Campopiano et al., 2014); Population is a numerical variable that is based on the de facto definition of population, which counts all residents regardless of legal status or citizenship -except for refugees not permanently settled in the country of asylum, who are generally considered part of the population of their country of origin. The values shown are midyear estimates; Market_Cap is a numerical variable that represents the share price times the number of shares outstanding. Listed domestic companies are the domestically incorporated companies listed on the country's stock exchanges at the end of the year. Listed companies do not include investment companies, mutual funds, or other collective investment vehicles. Data are in current U.S. dollars; Industry_GDP is a numerical variable that corresponds to ISIC divisions 10-45 and includes manufacturing (ISIC divisions 15-37). It comprises value added in mining, manufacturing (also reported as a separate subgroup), construction, electricity, water, and gas; R&D_GDP is a numerical variable that represents the expenditure on research and development in current and capital expenditure (both public and private) on creative work undertaken systematically to increase knowledge, including knowledge of humanity, culture, and society, and the use of knowledge for new applications. R&D covers basic research, applied research, and experimental development; Trade_GDP is a numerical variable that represents the sum of exports and imports of goods and services measured as a share of gross domestic product; $Industry_k$ are k dummy variables that represent the different k activity sectors in which the companies of the sample operate – i.e., energy, basic materials, industrial, construction, transportation and others; and $Year_t$ are t dummy variables that represent the t years of the sample, from 2002 to 2010.

*, **, and *** represent statistical significance at 95%, 99% and 99.9%, respectively.

Regarding the specific influence of family firms on this relationship, it should be noted that in our study sample, all of the largest companies in Canada, Italy, Japan, Spain and UK are family firms, and therefore the subsample of non-family firms contained no observations for the regression to be performed.

Furthermore, for the remaining countries analysed, there were insufficient observations for the non-family firms subsample, and so the regression of our model was not possible in this case either. Accordingly, in the regression for each country, the results are the same for the full sample as for the family firms subsample. In each of the nine countries, the added value generated by the largest family firms is associated with a higher rate of economic growth, a finding that corroborates previous results and our own research hypothesis. The highest Value_Added coefficient was recorded in Italy, and so the contribution of family firms to the added value achieved is particularly significant in this European country.

For the industry sector analysis, our findings provide evidence of the positive effect of added value on economic growth. In the subsample analysis, in some cases (Energy and Construction) there were insufficient observations to perform a regression of the model for the non-family-firm observations. Moreover, the Industrial, Transportation and "Others" sectors were only represented by family firms in our sample. Therefore, in these cases the results were the same for the full sample and for the family firms subsample.

However, on analysing the results for the family firms subsample, the findings for the activity sector analysis provide robust evidence complementing our previous results, reflecting a very positive effect on economic growth of the added value generated by family firms. According to this analysis, the added value generated by the largest companies in each country has a positive impact on the rate of economic growth in the sectors Energy, Basic Materials, Industrial and Transportation, and this effect is particularly significant for the family firms′ sample. For example, for the Basic Materials sample, Value_Added has a non-significant coefficient of 0.0000177 for the non-family firms′ subsample, while it has a positive (8.44E-06) and significant coefficient at a 99% confidence level for the family firms subsample. Moreover, this sector produced the highest coefficient, which may mean that the influence of family firms on economic growth is especially significant in this activity sector.

In our study, of family and non-family firms, the above findings reflect the positive influence on economic growth of the added value generated by the largest companies in each country, and in particular, the stronger influence of the value generated by family firms. This family firm influence is particularly significant in Italy and for the Basic Materials activity sector.

Conclusion

The aim of this chapter is to determine the existence or otherwise of a positive correlation between the added value generated by the largest companies and the economic growth achieved in their countries of origin. Specifically, we analyse the differences between family and non-family firms, concerning the contribution of their added value to national economic growth. Thus, the main purpose of this study is to highlight the contribution of family business to economic development worldwide.

To perform this study, we examined the 17 largest companies in each of nine countries (Canada, France, Germany, Italy, Japan, Hong Kong, Spain, UK and USA). Panel data techniques with a fixed effect were used to analyse the impact made by these companies on the rate of growth of GDP in their countries of origin. Thus, the analysis was performed globally, by country and by industry sector.

The results obtained show that a positive impact is made on the rate of economic growth by the added value generated by the largest companies in each country and, moreover, that family firms play a significant part in this impact. The positive influence exerted on rates of economic growth by the added value produced by these companies is especially significant among family firms, which highlights their influence on the economy and on the business community in general.

The present study contributes to previous research in several ways. On the one hand, we have extended understanding of the field, relating the added value generated by a group of companies in a country to the national rate of economic growth; and on the other hand, we have achieved a detailed understanding of the particular impact made by family business. As noted by Chrisman et al., (2003) and Gallo et al., (2004), among others, further research is needed to compare family and non-family business, to explain the competitive differences between these two forms of business organisation. In response, we have contributed by developing an empirical explanation of these differences and of their influence on the economic growth of leading countries. Moreover, this study analyses the impact made by family firms on national economic growth, and not only on their own performance.

In addition, this paper contributes to the existing literature on determinants of economic growth in other aspects. To date, studies have tended to focus on analysing determinants of a financial, economic, demographic or social nature (Hassan et al., 2011; Moral-Benito, 2012; Crespo-Cuaresma et al., 2014). In contrast, our own goal was to identify the types of ownership structure that most influence economic development at the national level, by addressing the relationship between economic growth and the added value generated by the family business. We make further contributions to this research field in our use of a sample of international data, applying a panel data methodology for the period 2002-2010. Instead of using cross-country samples, we examine a sample of various countries, thus extending the previous work conducted by Martikainen et al., (2009) with respect to US firms and that of Crespo-Cuaresma et al., (2014) on European regions. The use of panel data in regression analyses of economic growth represents an improvement on cross-country analysis alone, by avoiding the biases associated with cross-sectional regressions (Moral-Benito, 2012).

In sum, this study lays the foundation for continuing debate on changes in patterns of growth, with particular reference to the current economic situation. It is intended to encourage changes in the organisation and operation of businesses, and in the composition of economic activity and employment.

The results of this study may be of interest to various groups of users. On the one hand, our findings provide an opportunity for scholars and practitioners to further enhance our understanding of the relationship between family control and ownership and economic growth. The findings presented are also of special interest to the managers of family firms (highlighting opportunities for growth), to government institutions (regarding tax and legal issues concerning family businesses as creators of jobs and national wealth) and to society in general (in view of the impact of the economic and financial crisis and its effects on economic activity worldwide, producing a significant decline in economic growth, employment and living conditions).

The results of this study should be interpreted carefully. This research is subject to certain limitations, such as the way in which family firms are defined and measured, the non-inclusion of other variables that are also relevant to economic growth, the nature of the study sample, and the non-availability of databases with a greater volume of information for current periods of time. As areas for improvement, first, it would be better to consider family ownership and family management in greater detail, so as to better characterise the evidence discussed. The 'family firm' variable was dichotomised into family-controlled and non-family controlled firms, but as noted by Chen and Jaggi (2001) and Sharma (2004), without a continuous measure of this variable, the moderating effect of the family firm on the association between managerial discretion and entrenchment may not have been properly and fully evaluated. Second, it would be useful to include other variables related to economic growth and family business, such as media coverage, diversification, internalisation and the development of the capital market. Finally, our sample is biased, containing only nine countries. The evidence obtained needs to be expanded in future research, to address a wider range of countries which may present significant differences in their political, legal, cultural and socioeconomic environments. Nonetheless, we believe these limitations at the same time represent opportunities to advance and to better understand the link between family business and economic growth.

REFERENCES

Anderson, R. C., & Reeb, D. M. (2003). Founding-Family Ownership, Corporate Diversification, and Firm Leverage*. *Journal of Law and Economics,* 46(2), 653-684.

Arshad, R., & Razak, S. N. A. A. (2011). Corporate social responsibility disclosure and interaction effects of ownership structure on firm performance. In Business, Engineering and Industrial Applications (ISBEIA), *2011 IEEE Symposium on (pp. 111-116).* IEEE.

Astrachan, J.H., Klein, S.B., & Smyrnios, K.X. (2002). The F-PEC scale of family influence: A proposal for solving the family business definition problem. *Family Business Review* 15, 45–58.

Barth, E., Gulbrandsen, T., & Schønea, P. (2005). Family ownership and productivity: The role of owner-management. *Journal of Corporate Finance*, 11(1), 107-127.

Basu, N., Dimitrova, L., & Paeglis, I. (2009). Family control and dilution in mergers. *Journal of Banking & Finance*, 33(5), 829-841.

Berrone, P., Cruz, C., Gómez Mejía, L.R., & LarrazaKintana, M. (2010). Socio-emotional wealth and corporate responses to institutional pressures: Do family-controlled firms pollute less? *Administrative Science Quarterly,* 55(1): 82-113.

Bueno, J. C. C., Navarro, J. L. B., & Menéndez, A. M. M. (2013). Reestructuración y tipo de propiedad en empresas en crisis. Diferencias entre empresas familiar y no familiares. *Revista de Empresa Familiar,* 3(1), 7-20.

Campopiano, G., De Massis, A., & Chirico, F. (2014). Firm philanthropy in small-and medium-sized family firms: the effects of family involvement in ownership and management. *Family Business Review*, 27(3), 244-258.

Chen, C. J. & Jaggi, B. (2001). Association between independent non-executive directors, family control and financial disclosures in Hong Kong. *Journal of Accounting and Public Policy*, 19(4), 285-310.

Chrisman, J. J., Chua, J. H., & Steier, L. P. (2003). An introduction to theories of family business. Journal of Business Venturing, 18(4), 441-448.

Chua, J., Chrisman, J.J., & Sharma, P. (1999). Defining the family business by behavior. Entrepreneurship: Theory & Practice, Summer: 19-39.

Ciccone, A. & Jarocinski, M. (2010). Determinants of economic growth: will data tell? *American Economic Journal: Macroeconomics*, 2: 223-247.

Crespo-Cuaresma, J., Doppelhofer, G. & Feldkircher, M. (2014). Determinants of economic growth in European Regions. Regional Studies, 48(1): 44-67.

Curasi, C. F., Price, L. L., & Arnould, E. J. (2004). How individuals' cherished possessions become families' inalienable wealth. *Journal of Consumer Research*, 31(3), 609-622.

De Massis, A., Sharma, P., Chua, J. H., & Chrisman, J. J. (2012). Family business studies: An annotated bibliography. Edward Elgar Publishing.

Duréndez, A., García, D. & Madrid, A. (2007a). "Professionally Managed Family Firms", In V. Gupta, N. Levenburg, L. Moore, J. Motwani, & Schwarz, Thomas (eds.). A Compendium on the Family Business Models Around the World, Hyderabad: ICFAI University Press, (Forthcoming), 1-21.

Durlauf, S., Johnson, P., & Temple, J. (2005). Growth Econometrics (Vol. 1A: 555-577), In Aghion, P. & Duraluf, S.N. (Eds). *Handbook of Economic Growth* (Amsterdam, North-Holland, 2005).

Eddleston, K. A., & Kellermanns, F. W. (2007). Destructive and productive family relationships: A stewardship theory perspective. *Journal of Business Venturing*, 22(4), 545-565.

Esparza-Aguilar, J.L., García-Pérez de Lema, D., & Duréndez, A. (2009). Gestión Financiera y Sistemas de Control de Gestión en las MIPYME Familiares: Un Estudio Empírico en el Sector Turístico Mexicano.

Gallo, M. Á., Tàpies, J., & Cappuyns, K. (2004). Comparison of family and nonfamily business: Financial logic and personal preferences. *Family Business Review*, 17(4), 303-318.

Gomez-Mejia, L. R., Nunez-Nickel, M., & Gutierrez, I. (2001). The role of family ties in agency contracts. *Academy of Management Journal*, 44(1), 81-95.

Green, W. H. (1999). *Econometric analysis*. Madrid: Prentice Hall.

Habbershon, T., & Williams, M. (1999). A resource-based framework for assessing the strategic advantages of family firms. *Family Business Review*, 12: 1-25.

Hassan, M. K., Sanchez, B., & Yu, J. S. (2011). Financial development and economic growth: New evidence from panel data. *The Quarterly Review of Economics and Finance*, 51(1), 88-104.

Kashmiri, S. & Mahajan, V. 2010. What's in a name?: An analysis of the strategic behavior of family firms. *International Journal of Research in Marketing,* 27(3), 271-280.

Kim, E. (2006). The impact of family ownership and capital structures on productivity performance of Korean manufacturing firms: Corporate governance and the "chaebol problem". *Journal of the Japanese and International Economies*, 20(2), 209-233.

La Porta, R., Lopez-de-Silanes, F. & Shleifer, A. (2002). Government ownership of banks. *The Journal of Finance*, 57(1), 265-301.

Lee, Y. (2006). Diagnostic testing for dynamic panel data models, The 14th Conference on Panel Data, 2007. http://www.wise.xmu.edu.cn/panel2007/paper/LEE(Yoon-Jin).pdf.

Lyagoubi, M. (2006). 29 Family firms and financial behavior: how family shareholder preferences influence firms' financing. *Handbook of Research on Family Business,* 537.

Madura, C. C., & Ronquillo, C. C. (2008). Determinantes del crecimiento económico e intermediación bancaria: un análisis empírico para países latinoamericanos. *Panorama Socioeconómico*, (37), 108-119.

Martikainen, M., Nikkinen, J., & Vähämaa, S. (2009). Production functions and productivity of family firms: Evidence from the S&P 500. *The Quarterly Review of Economics and Finance*, 49(2), 295-307.

Maury, B. (2006). Family ownership and firm performance: Empirical evidence from Western European corporations. *Journal of Corporate Finance*, 12(2), 321-341.

Moral-Benito, E. (2012). Determinants of economic growth: A Bayesian panel data approach. *The Review of Economics and Statistics*, 94(2): 566-579.

Moreno, A. M., & Casillas, J. C. (2008). Entrepreneurial orientation and growth of SMEs: A causal model. *Entrepreneurship Theory and Practice,* 32(3), 507-528.

Nicholson, N. (2008). Evolutionary psychology and family business: A new synthesis for theory, research, and practice. *Family Business Review*, 21(1), 103-118.

Peteraf, M. A. & Barney, J. B. (2003). Unraveling the resource-based tangle. *Managerial and Decision Economics*, 24: 309-323.

Pindado, J., & Requejo, I. (2012). Panel data: a methodology for model specification and testing. Finance volume of Wiley Encyclopedia of Management.

Sánchez, A. F. J. (2013). Desarrollo del sector servicios y su papel en la consolidación del crecimiento económico mundial. *Ecos de Economía,* 17(36), 43-68.

Sharma, P. (2004). An overview of the field of family business studies: Current status and directions for the future. *Family Business Review*, 17(1), 1-36.

Shleifer, A., & Vishny, R. W. (1997). A survey of corporate governance. *The Journal of Finance*, 52(2), 737-783.

Sirmon, D., & Hitt, M. (2003). Managing resources: Linking unique resources, management, and wealth creation in family firms. *Entrepreneurship Theory and Practice*, 27: 339-358.

Uhlaner, L. M. (2005). The use of the Guttman Scale in development of a Damily Orientation Index for Small-to-Medium-Size Firms. *Family Business Review,* 18: 41-56.

Zahra, S. A., Priem, R. L. & Rasheed, A. A. (2005). The antecedents and consequences of top management fraud. *Journal of Management* 31(6): 803-828.

In: Financial Performance
Editor: Elaine Moreno
ISBN: 978-1-63484-501-4

Chapter 2

CEO DUALITY AND FIRM PERFORMANCE IN NIGERIA: IMPLICATION FOR FAMILY OWNED FIRMS

Augustine Ujunwa* and Chinwe Okoyeuzu†
Department of Banking and Finance, University of Nigeria,
Enugu Campus, Enugu, Nigeria

ABSTRACT

Manuscript type: Empirical

Purpose: The purpose of this study is to empirically determine whether the one-rule-fits-all approached adopted by the Nigerian Securities Exchange Commission in terms of the separation of board chairman form the CEO promotes firm performance irrespective of the firms' ownership structures, in Nigerian with strong dominance of family owned firms.

Design/methodology/approach: The study is restricted to firms quoted on the Nigerian Stock Exchange. Pooled data for 18-years period 1994-2011 were collated from published annual reports and statement of accounts of 91 ownership dispersed firms and 72 ownership concentrated firms. Two equation system Ordinary Least Square multiple regressions were used to estimate the relationship between firm financial performance and CEO duality along ownership structures in Nigeria.

* Email: austinesilver@yahoo.com, Tel: +2348035010116
† Email:chinwe.okoyeuzu@unn.edu.ng, Tel: +2347038599237

Findings: The findings of the study showed that while board duality was negative in predicting the financial performance of ownership dispersed firms; same cannot be said of ownership concentrated firms (family owned firms) as duality was found to be positive in predicting financial performance.

Research Limitations/Implications: Paucity of substantial local literature on institutional perspective of agency constitutes the major limitation of this study. Although, this study is meant to close this gap, the implication is that foreign theoretical and empirical literature standpoint constitutes the bulk of the review, which may not explain reasons for any identifiable local trends in Nigeria.

Practical Implication: The study reveals the importance of taking into cognizance, institutional perspective of agency theory in solving the excess power assigned to the board of directors, especially for family owned firms, where the family members have strong incentive to monitor the managers.

Originality/Value: This study contributes to the institutional perspective of agency theory from Nigerian institutional perspective. The study revealed the importance of accommodating individual country specificities in draft corporate governance laws.

Keywords: Agency Theory, Corporate Governance, Firm Performance

INTRODUCTION

Corporate governance has received enormous interest among policy makers, industry players and scholars from early nineties till date (Cadbury, 1992). Interest on corporate governance has accentuated in recent time because of the corporate scandals in different countries such as Paramalat in Italy, Enron, Tyco International in the United States, WorldCom, HIH Insurance in Australia (France and Carney, 2002; Bosner and Fisher, 2007, Byron, 2007). Second, the 2007/2008 global financial crisis that ravaged the global financial architect and undermines the fundamental economic and political ideologies of nations has shown the importance of corporate governance in preventing systemic disruptions (Canadian Office of the Superintendent of Financial Institutions, 2008; Rodger, 2008).

The enactment of Sarbanes-Oxley Act of 2012 could be attributed to the public outcry after the Enron collapse (Moeller, 2004) with the objective of improving the oversight functions of the board and ensures compliance. Other countries also evinced keen interest on the role of boards and governance. For example, the UK commissioned different reports to make boards and governance effective. These include Cadbury report on the financial aspects of corporate governance (1992), Greenbury report on directors' remuneration (1995), Hampel report on corporate governance (1998), Turnbull report on guidance for directors (1999), Higgs report on role and effectiveness of non-executive directors (2003), Tyson Report on recruitment and development of non-executive directors (2003) and Combined Code on corporate governance (2003). Italy has issued Preda Code (2002) for self regulation by listed firms while South Africa released King Report on corporate governance (2002). Also, CLSA, a Hong Kong based investment banker, started publishing a regular report on Corporate Governance in collaboration with Asian Corporate Governance Association (ACGA) since 2000. This report covers all major firms in the Emerging Markets of Asia, Latin America, Europe, Middle East and Africa.

Most corporate governance codes in developing economies, especially Africa, adopted the Anglo-Saxon corporate governance model, characterized by financing through equity, dispersed ownership, active markets for corporate control, and flexible labour markets dispersed, strong legal regulation, and where contractual incentives are key governance mechanisms (Descender, 2009). Anglo-Saxon model is usually described as typical traditional version of corporate governance approach in United States and United Kingdom.

However, recent studies have begun exploring differences between United States and United Kingdom approaches to governance that have traditionally been treated together as the Anglo-American model, commonly described as bank-based economies (Aguilera, Williams, Conley and Rupp, 2006; Toms and Wright, 2005; Williams and Conley, 2005). These findings of the studies show no great difference in terms of the social purpose of regulation in the United States and the United Kingdom as there is between shareholder and stakeholder models on the question of corporate social responsibility. The major difference between U.S. and U.K. corporate governance, however, lies in the regulatory methods and styles adopted by each country. According to Kaga (2001), more prescriptive regulatory approach of the United States that is based on a formal legalism in the context of a litigation culture stands in contrast to the principles-based approach of the United Kingdom.

The Anglo-Saxon model is in line with the agency theory which argues that managers with superior knowledge and expertise about firms can pursue self-serving behavior to the detriment of shareholders interest (Fama and Jensen, 1983). Jensen and Meckling (1976) assume that such "agency problem can be resolved with appropriately designed contracts by specifying the rights belonging to agents and principals".

The Nigerian Securities and Exchange Commission (SEC) set-up a Corporate Governance Committee on June 15^{t}, 2000 to review corporate governance laws for quoted companies in Nigeria. The committee submitted its report which was titled "Code of Best Practices for Public Companies in Nigeria". The report was adopted in 2003 and perceived as international best corporate governance practices. The Code was however reviewed in 2011 and re-christened "Code of Corporate Governance in Nigeria 2011 and International Best Practices on Corporate Governance" though not in the public domain yet. The Code retained some recommendations of the 2003 Codes such as; (a) the composition of the board which favours the dominance of non-executive directors; (b) the separation of the position and responsibilities of the board chairman and the chief executive officer; (3) that quality information should be provided to the board in a timely manner; (4) clear cut procedure for the appointment of new directors which must be formal and transparent; (5) objective and reliable financial reporting; and (6) instutionalisation of sound and robust internal control system.

This policy prescription enshrined in the Nigerian corporate governance code which was defined as universal best practice, relies extensively on the Anglo-Saxon model that is largely influence by agency theory. Millar et al. (2005) are of the argue "that country specific such as ownership structure, the enforceability of corporate regulations and culture, and diverse corporate governance mechanism need to be taken into cognizance in formulating functional corporate governance codes for any country". In Nigerian, corporate environment is characterized by dispersed and concentrated ownership structures, controlled and managerial ownership, and family ownership of firms. An important research question is, whether all Nigerian firms, irrespective of their ownership structure, should be subjected to the 'one-rule-fits all' of separation of CEO and the chairman, given the advocacy that compliance to the code should be made compulsory. That is, should family owned firms, with concentrated ownership structure, strong incentive to monitor management, be subjected to separating board chair from CEO, even where such arrangement increases agency cost and contributes negatively to the firm financial performance?

The objective of this study is to address the above question. Despite the mixed results in empirical literature on the link between CEO duality and firm performance in different jurisdiction (Dalton et al. (1998), policy makers are favourably disposed to prescribing the separation of CEO from the board chair as one of the best strategies for resolving agency conflicts between agents and principals. Nigerian corporate regulators also fell into such euphoria by issuing calls to dismantle the practice of CEO duality in the entire spectrum of Nigerian corporate environment (SEC, 2003, 2011). The decision to dismantle the practice of CEO duality in line with the agency theory without concrete empirical evidence motivated the researchers to investigate Nigerian institutional perspective to agency theory. Specifically, the study uses Nigerian data to examine the impact of CEO-duality on firm performance for dispersed and family owned firm. To achieve this, the rest of the paper is structured as follow; section 2 reviews of related literature and hypotheses formulation. Section 4 discusses the methodology, and section 5 discusses the results, while section 5 concludes the paper.

Literature Review

Poor corporate performance has caused a major drop in shareholder value in most developing economy in general and Nigeria in particular. It is widely accepted that board composition plays a vital role in determining the financial performance of a firm. It is very obvious that corporate governance structure of a firm has critical impact on its performance. In corporate governance discourse, board of director is an important element, most especially in developing countries. Agency theorists have identified boards of directors as a primary monitoring device protecting shareholder interests. Boards of directors are charged with ensuring that chief executive officers (CEOs) carry out their duties in a way that serves the best interests of shareholders. The role of corporate board is considered more important in such economies because of the relative weakness in governance mechanism and institutions.

Most studies on corporate governance are influenced by the agency theory. Agency theory argues that since corporate managers are not owners but agents of the owners, contracted to manage the firm on behalf of the owners, they have less personal wealth at stake, and "their natural pursuit of self interest could result in them taking riskier or even dishonest actions, which could bring harm to the firm or its owners" (Bosner, 2007; Jensen and Meckling, 1976). Proponents of this theory supported independent board, and argued for the "separation of the position of the CEO from the board chair".

Agency theorists view the function of corporate board as that of monitoring the actions of agents in order to protect the principal (Eisenhardt, 1989). Decender (2009) argues that "monitoring by the board is important because of the potential cost incurred when management pursues its own interest at the expense of shareholders' interest". Agency theorists posit that monitoring by boards of directors can reduce agency cost inherent in the separation of ownership and control and, in this way improve firm performance (Fama, 1980; Zahra and Pearce, 1989).

Whether CEO duality, the practice of having one person as firm's CEO and board chair contributes to firm performance is probably a controversial and inconclusive question in corporate governance research and practice. CEO duality has opposing effects that boards must attempt to balance. The proponents of CEO duality documents the utility value of having one person perform the role of the chairman and that of the CEO. For instance, they argue that duality connotes clear leadership structure, definition of responsibilities, which leads to increase effectiveness and improved performance (Fox, 1998; and Donalson and Davis, 1991). Anderson and Anthony (1986) argue that "the separation of board chair and CEO roles is guaranteed to produce chaos both within the organization and in relationships with the board". In their view, "such chaos is likely to have a negative effect on the formulation of corporate strategy and the responsiveness of the company to changes in the environment". These factors according to Fox (1998) have the "inherent capacity of promoting poor corporate financial performance".

However, opponents of CEO duality argue that duality could lead poor performance due to the selfish interest of powerful managers, especially, where the role of the board is compromised. The second argument against CEO duality centered on the relative role expectation of each proposed by Changanti, et al. (1985). They argue that "a company CEO is involved in the day-to-day running of the organization, while the board chair is often involved in special planning assignments, in policy review and formulation, and in public and stockholder relations". Since the CEO is involved in the day-to-day running of the organization, he may not be able to perform the additional roles of chairperson effectively. Stewart (1991) also documented the roles of board chair as monitoring – "acting as coach and counselor, positively seeking to influence the [CEOs] behaviours", and consultant – "giving advice to the CEO and other directors". As such, excessive concentration of the powers on one person may influence the financial performance of the firm negatively. Agency theory is very clear in its position regarding CEO duality. This is from the standpoint that CEO indicates nonexistence of separation of decision management and decision control. According to agency theory, duality promotes CEO entrenchment by reducing board monitoring efficiency.

Peng, Zhang and Li (2007) investigated the impact of CEO duality of firm financial performance. Their results based on archival database covering 403 publicly listed Chinese firms, found that CEO duality promotes firm financial performance. Sridharam and Marsinko (1997) also investigated the impact of CEO duality on the market value of the firm using paper and forest product industry, over the period: 1988-1992. Their result showed that firms with CEO duality have "superior performance in terms of margins and productive utilization of assets which is reflected in a higher market value of the firm". Also, Dey, Engel and Liu (2009) examine the determinants and performance of board leadership structure. Their result showed that firms with greater information flows, stronger governance and more powerful CEO are likely to have a leadership structure that combines the CEO and the chair roles. Their result showed that dual firms with greater net benefits from combining these roles outperform firms with separate roles.

However, Chen et al. (2008) findings showed that there is no significant relationship between CEO duality and firm performance. Norman, Iskandar and Rahmat (2005) investigate the effectiveness of some board characteristics to monitor management behaviour with respect to their incentives to manage earnings. The result shows that the ratio of independent board members is not significantly related to earnings management in firms with duality status. Hambrick and D'Aveni's (1992) used 57 bankrupt and 57 survivors firms to investigate board structure as a determinant of bankruptcy. Their findings showed that CEO dominance was significant predictor of bankruptcy.

These studies are in developed countries where the external governance environment and institutions that support the internal firm governance are stable and well developed (Singh and Gaur, 2009). Though the studies has advanced our understanding of the link between governance structure and firm performance, it is important to state that the efficiency of the internal governance mechanisms in the developed economies depend on the quality of external governance and institutions, which would have influenced the results (Peng et al. 2007). This is particularly important for Nigeria that lacks the institutions needed to promote efficient internal firm governance. For instance, Nigeria does not have well developed external control mechanism such as market for corporate control, mergers and acquisition laws, and efficient law enforcement to support internal governance laws.

The unique nature of the Nigerian corporate environment influenced the researchers to investigate the impact of CEO duality on firm performance using an integration of the agency theory within the institutional perspective. Specifically, we investigate two aspects of firm institutional perspectives in

Nigeria (ownership structures) – disperse ownership and family owned firm (with concentrated ownership). In doing so, this paper contributes to the governance literature, by providing a more holistic theoretical framework and empirical findings in developing economies.

In the Nigerian corporate environment, there are 212 public companies under 37 industrial classifications as at 2010 which where collapsed into 13 industries in 2011 in order to comply with the global standard. However, this study adopted the 2010 classification because of the low compliance rate to the new paradigm and paucity of data under the new paradigm. The classification include, airline services, agriculture/agro-allied, automobile and tire, banking, aviation, breweries, chemicals and paints, building materials, conglomerates, commercial/services, construction, engineering technology, emerging markets, food/beverages and tobacco, healthcare, footwear, hotel and tourism, industrial/domestic products, information communication and telecommunication, insurance, leasing, machinery (marketing), maritime, media, mortgage companies, memorandum quotations, other financial institutions, packaging, petroleum marketing, printing and publishing, real estate, real estate investment trust, road transportation, textiles and foreign listing.

Apart from industries like banking, petroleum marketing, conglomerate, and food/beverages and tobacco that have some degree of foreign and dispersed ownership structure, other industries are predominantly family owned businesses. These family owned firms have the characteristics of being young, small in terms of asset size, concentrated ownership structure and strong family influence or ties.

Thus, ownership structure is an important feature of the Nigerian corporate environment, and has thrived due to policy inducement and institutional voids. The principles of company laws in Nigeria were derived from English law, which could be traced to the influence of colonization. Also, the early companies that operated in Nigeria were British based companies. After independence from the colonial rule in 1960, the Nigerian government responded to the agitation that the Nigerian economy was dominated by direct foreign capital investment, by the promulgating the Nigerian Enterprise Promotion Decree of 1972 (also known as the Indigenization Decree of 1972 amended in 1977), which was targeted at promoting indigenous participation in industrial activities, This policy inducement created strong family hegemony as some ethnic tribes in Nigeria had better advantage in acquiring the indigenized firms over others. This was compounded by the conspicuous absence of institutions needed for efficient functioning of public corporations at that time.

Additionally, with explicit sub-optimal functioning of public corporations and the adoption of Structural Adjustment Programme (SAP) the government succumbed to the international pressure of privatizing public corporations. The Bureau for Public Enterprise (the official vehicle for privatization) which was saddled with corrupt politicians and their cronies saw the sale as their own share of national cakes, and sold the companies to themselves, family relatives and friend at a rate that is far below the market rate. This institutional void also promoted family firms in Nigeria.

STATEMENT OF HYPOTHESES

In our first hypothesis, we argue that for firms with dispersed ownership structure, shareholders do not have the incentive to monitor managers individually, since they do not have sufficient incentives (payoff) to expand resources on monitoring the managerial or agents' behaviour. Agency problem therefore will arise because (a) "the desires or goal of the principal and agent conflicts and"; (b) "it is difficult for the principal to verify what the agent is actually doing". This problem accentuated because of weak external governance, which not only incentive managers to deliberately embark on self-serving behaviour than the overall wellbeing of the affected firms, but also allow them get away with loose adherence to rules to the detriment of their principal.

The self-serving behavior pursuit by agents increase the costs to the firm, which may include the costs of restructuring contacts, cost of monitoring and controlling the behaviour of the agents, and loss incurred due to sub-optimal decisions taken by the agents. As such, the most effective way to mitigate this agency problem is to have an independent board that separates the position of the board chair from the CEO. Consequently, any corporate leadership structure that merges the position of board chair and CEO (board duality) is expected to have negative impact on firm performance. Accordingly, we hypothesize;

Hypothesis 1: CEO duality will have negative effect on financial performance of ownership dispersed firms in Nigeria.

For the second hypothesis, we argue that the Nigerian corporate governance laws and governance standards are not strong in spite of the progress made in recent years.

The stock market is not developed, and firms are still learning effective strategies for operating in such a volatile economy. Families are unwilling to relinquish their controlling shares because of the fringe benefits they enjoy and still strive to ensure that the family maintains higher stake in the company through pre-emptive rights (in line Company and Allied Matters Act 1990 as amended, pre-emptive rights allow existing shareholders to subscribe a certain percentage of shares that is proportionate to the percentage of their initial shareholding in a company before issuing to other members of the public). In concentrated ownership (family owned firms), agency problem is reduced since the concentrated shareholders can effectively influence and monitor management, sometimes by personally sitting on the board. Shleifer and Vishny (1986) argue "that large shareholders have strong incentives to monitor managers because of their significant economic stakes. In such arrangement, the board may be designed to assist management".

The presence of CEO on the board will be beneficial, as it will improve the information flow towards the board members (Descender, 2009). We expect that if the CEO is also the chairman of the board, the interaction and discussion of the CEO with the board members may lead to more valuable advice and better financial performance and any legislation that disrupts this arrangement will increase the agency cost. For instance, owners/managers of firms may view board independence as a mere statutory requirements and attempt to fill it by appointing people who considers their role ceremonial. Accordingly, we hypothesize;

Hypothesis 2: CEO duality has positive effect on the financial performance of ownership concentrated (family owned) firms in Nigeria.

DATA AND METHODOLOGY

Data and Sample

The study employed firm-level data collated from annual reports and statement of accounts of publicly quoted companies on Nigerian Stock Exchange (without any restrictions for tier one and tier two markets) and the Nigerian stock Exchange statistical yearbooks. These sources are updated from the African Financials.com database.

Ironically, outside the Thompson DataStream that has data for a few African countries; no other global economics/business database has consistent corporate data on African firms. The study covers the period 1994-2011.

Restrictions were imposed on the sample as firms without six years missing observations were omitted from the sample. Based on this criterion, 91 firms representing 87% of the total firms were selected for ownership dispersed firms. Also, 72 firms representing 79% of the total firms were selected for family owned (ownership concentrated) firms. Firm were classified as family firms or concentrated ownership firms if the proportion of common stock held by top twenty shareholders constitute at least fifty one percent of total shares or within extended or nuclear family members and dispersed ownership structure if otherwise.

Analytical Approach

The two hypotheses were estimated with two equation system in line with the work Seifert and Gonenc (2012). The equations take follows forms for the two corporate ownership structures;

$$PBIT\_TA = C_o + C_1 BDuality + C_2 LogSize + C_3 LogAge + e - \qquad (1)$$

where *PBIT_TA* is profit before interest and tax divided by total assets; *Bduality* is board duality, a dummy variable that takes the value of 1 if the same person is the board chairman and CEO, and 0 if otherwise (Chancharat, Krishnamurti and Tian, 2012); *LogSize* is natural logarithm of board size which entered as controlled variable; and *LogAge*, the natural logarithm of firm age proxied by number of years from date of incorporation, which also entered as controlled variable.

To ensure that unobserved heterogeneity is not correlated with the independent variables, we applied fixed and random-effect estimation (Stock and Watson, 2007). Results of the tests showed some significant support for the fixed effects regression than the random effects (See Figures 1, 2 and 3 for details of the fixed effects, random effects and Hausmam test results in the appendix).

The hypotheses were estimated using the Fixed-Effects Generalised Least Square (GLS) unbalanced firm-level panel data for the period 1994-201.

Variable	Observations	Mean	Std. Dev	Minimum	Maximum
BDuality	2078	.4456208	.4971537	0	1
LogTA	1868	5.607853	1.076507	1.52	9.09
ROAE	1924	.2478586	8.351945	-281.55	213.5
LogAge	2041	1.458702	.2479898	0	2.37

Source: Computed from Handpicked Data (Using Stata-Computa Analytical Package).

Figure 1. Descriptive Statistics of Ownership Dispersed Firm.

Variable	Observations	Mean	Std. Dev	Minimum	Maximum
BDuality	688	.7194767	.4246053	0	1
LogTA	658	6.307153	1.080093	1.785	9.455
ROAE	681	.4636138	6.798239	-13.443	162.727
LogAge	662	1.441956	.2867659	0	1.886

Source: Computed from Handpicked Data (Using Stata-Computa Analytical Package).

Figure 2. Descriptive Statistics of Ownership Concentrated Firms.

Variable	BDuality	LogTA	ROAE	LogAge
BDuality	1.0000			
LogTA	-0.0319	1.0000		
ROAE	0.0221	0.0685*	1.0000	
LogAge	-0.0064	0.0794*	0.0265	1.000

*correlation is significant at the 0.05 level (2-tailed).

Source: Computed from Handpicked Data (Using Stata-Computa Analytical Package)

Figure 3. Correlation Matrix of Ownership Dispersed Firms.

Variables and Measures

The dependent variable is profit before interest and tax divided by total assets (return on asset employed). Though there have been serious controversies regarding what constitutes corporate financial performance (example,Cochran and Wood, 1984). Return on asset employed is an indicator of what management has accomplished with the given resources (assets), and according to agency theory, managers are likely to squander profits and misappropriate earnings, leaving lesser returns for shareholders. A lower return on assets will indicate inefficiency. The independent variable CEO-duality is a corporate leadership structure that merges the position of board chair and CEO. CEO duality is measured by a dummy variable BDuality which takes the value of 1 if the CEO and chairman are the same person and 0 if the CEO is separated from the board chairman (Chancharat, Krishnamurti and Tian, 2012). Two controlled variables were included in the model. This choice is influenced by prior empirical literature. First is firm size, since is it generally argued that as the complexity of a firm increase, the internal structure changes due to need for monitoring (Booth et al. 2002; Peasnell et al. 2003; Pfeffer, 1972; and Zahra and Pearce, 1989). Thus, as firm size increases, the agency costs are expected to increase since a large span allows for greater managerial discretion and opportunism, resulting in increased monitoring (Jensen and Meckling, 1976). Total asset was used as a proxy for firm size and measured by the natural logarithm of total assets. Second is firm age, which is the number of years for which a firm has been in operation, starting with the date of incorporation. New firms are expected to have smaller earnings than old ones because they have less experience in the market, are still building their market position, and normally have a higher costs structure (Berger and Udell, 1998; Gregory et al. 2005; and Lipczinsky and Wilson, 2001). This is measured as the natural logarithm of age since incorporation. Table 1 list all the variables used and their exact definitions.

Table 1. Operational Definition of Variables

Variables	Notation	Operational Definitions	Proxies
Firm Performance	ROA	Return on Asset Employed	*PBIT/Total Assets*
Firm Size	LogTA	Log of Total Assets	*LogTA*
Firm Age	LogAge	Log of Years since Incorporation	*LogAge*
CEO Duality	BDuality	If the Same Person is Chairman and CEO 1 If the Chairman is Separate from the CEO 0	*Bduality*

RESULTS

Descriptive Statistics

Board duality is a dummy variable taking the value of 1 if the manager of the firm is also the chairman and 0 if otherwise. The result from table 2 showed that 76% of the firms in the observations separated the position of CEO from the board chair, while 24% of the selected firms allowed one person to function simultaneously as manager and board chairman for ownership dispersed firms.

The descriptive statistics results in table 3 show that 28% of the selected firms separate the position of CEO from board chair, while 72% of the selected firms merged the two positions for family firms. The results did not contradict theoretical arguments that as firms get older and larger, they separate the position of CEO from the board chairman in order to ensure effectively monitoring of management. The results from the descriptive statistics also supported our *a priori* expectation that ownership dispersed firms are naturally inclined to separating the CEO position from board chair to mitigate the agency problem, while ownership family owned firms normally allow for the unification of these two positions since their large stake in the firm gives the incentive to monitor management self-serving behaviour.

Considering the accounting measure of return on asset, it is found that the average return on assets is approximately 25% for ownership dispersed firms and 46% for ownership concentrated firms. The interpretation of this result is somewhat slippery.

Table 2. Descriptive Statistics of Ownership Dispersed Firm

Variable	Observations	Mean	Std. Dev	Minimum	Maximum
BDuality	2078	.2356208	.2871537	0	1
LogTA	1868	5.607853	1.076507	1.52	9.09
ROAE	1924	.2478586	8.351945	-281.55	213.5
LogAge	2041	1.458702	.2479898	0	2.37

Source: Computed from Handpicked Data (Using Stata-Computa Analytical Package).

Table 3. Descriptive Statistics of Ownership Concentrated Firms

Variable	Observations	Mean	Std. Dev	Minimum	Maximum
BDuality	688	.7194767	.4246053	0	1
LogTA	658	6.307153	1.080093	1.785	9.455
ROAE	681	.4636138	6.798239	-13.443	162.727
LogAge	662	1.441956	.2867659	0	1.886

Source: Computed from Handpicked Data (Using Stata-Computa Analytical Package).

The result suggests that smaller firms outperform larger firms in terms of return on asset employed. This result might have been influenced by the measure used. For example, profit before interest and tax ignores the tax re-bate which large firms enjoy as result of their collateral value and degree of leverage. Generally, the result is interpreted to suggest that managers effectively manage the assets of the companies in terms of converting them into income.

However, one common trend among the companies is the fact that approximately 75 per cent of board chair are occupied by a retired Army General or persons connected to the government. This shows a strong case of crony capitalism in the Nigerian corporate environment. Crony capitalism is an economic system which the allocation of resources and the adjudication of commercial disputes are generally made in favour of those who have a close relationship with political leaders or government officials, by blood (nepotism) or by bribes (corruption) (Vaugirard, 2004).

Most board chairmen in Nigeria are retired military generals, ex-ministers and relations of ex-Nigerian leaders. This arrangement allows well-connected economic agents to earn returns above those that would prevail in an economy which the factors of production were priced by the market. Firms use these cronies to attract government patronage and shield themselves from the axe of the law.

Correlation Results

Table 4 and 5 present the correlation matrixes of ownership dispersed firms and ownership concentrated firms respectively.

The correlations between firm age and return on assets employed are weakly positive for both ownership structures. Though the non-significant relationship may create the impression that these two variables are not important, but the arising statistics tend to prove that the age of the firm has a positive relationship with the profitability of the firm, and justifies the inclusion of the variable as control variable. Most of the coefficients, as observed, whether positive or negative, significant or non-significant are weak. This indicates at first glance, that although likely cases of multicolinearity may exist, the degree of such may be too remote to affect the results of the regression estimates.

Table 4. Correlation Matrix of Ownership Dispersed Firms

Variable	BDuality	LogTA	ROAE	LogAge
BDuality	1.0000			
LogTA	-0.0319	1.0000		

ROAE	0.0221	0.0685*	1.0000	
LogAge	-0.0064	0.0794*	0.0265	1.000

*correlation is significant at the 0.05 level (2-tailed).

Table 5. Correlation Matrix of Ownership Dispersed Firms

Variable	BDuality	LogTA	ROAE	LogAge
BDuality	1.0000			
LogTA	-0.0176	1.0000		
ROAE	-0.0267	-0.1015	1.0000	
LogAge	0.0851	-0.1035	0.0095	1.000

*correlation is significant at the 0.05 level (2-tailed).

Regression Results

Table 6 and 7 presents the regression results. The coefficient of CEO duality (see table 6) was negative and non-significant in predicting the financial performance ownership dispersed firms. This result re-enforces the theoretical underpinning of the board's monitoring function derived from agency theory, which describes the potential for conflict of interest that arises from the separation of ownership and control in organizations (Fama and Jensen, 1983). Agency theorists see the primary function of boards as monitoring the actions of "agents"- managers - to protect the interests of "principals" -owners (Jensen and Meckling, 1976). Monitoring by the board is important because of the potential costs incurred when management pursues its own interests at the expense of shareholders' interests. Monitoring by boards of directors can reduce agency costs inherent in the separation of ownership and control and, in this way, improve firm performance.

However, the coefficient of CEO duality was positive but not significant in predicting the financial performance of family owned firms. This result implies that board duality is desirable for family owned firms that are young in terms of firm age, relatively small in term of asset size and with concentrated ownership structure. This is a very consistent result with our a priori expectation considering that CEO duality may be beneficial for a young firm if the board of directors is designed to assist management. Not only will his(her) presence improve the information flow towards the board members, but the interaction and discussion of the CEO with board members may lead to more valuable advice and better firm performance. This re-enforces the preposition that governance arrangement aimed at resolving the excess power of the board should take into cognizance the institutional perspectives of the countries.

Table 6. GLS Regression for Ownership Dispersed Firms

.regress LogPBIT_TA BDual LogTA LogAge						
LogPBIT-TA	Coef.	Std Err.	t	P>/t/	[95% Conf	Interval]
BDual	-.1578114	.1022893	-1.54	0.123	-.3584303	.0428075
LogTA	-.1060291	.0478133	-2.22	0.027	-.1998048	-.0122534
LogAge	.3319436	.2088508	1.59	0.112	-.0776733	.7415605
_con	-.4515175	.3907606	1.14	0.255	-.3266228	1.22968

Table 7. GLS Regression for Ownership Dispersed Firms

.regress LogPBIT_TA BDual LogTA LogAge						
LogPBIT-TA	Coef.	Std Err.	t	P>/t/	[95% Conf	Interval]
BDual	.1489808	.2643398	0.56	0.573	.6680825	.3701209
LogTA	-.1668431	.1046516	-1.59	0.111	-.3723544	-.0386683
LogAge	.557649	.394295	0.14	0.888	-.7197846	.8313144
_con	1.231439	.9199554	1.34	0.181	.5751391	3.038017

CONCLUSION

The unique context of emerging economies raises empirical questions, as the governance arrangements found in these countries are quite different from those found in developed countries. For example, firms often arrange themselves in the form of business groups through pyramidal ownership in countries that lack the institutions needed for efficient market based financial system. Such governance arrangements may make traditional governance mechanism, such as the presence of board chairman redundant. The board chairman may be ceremonial, and therefore may not be effective, and their role may be limited to satisfying the statutory requirements which increases agency cost (Zajac and Westphal, 1996).

The findings of the study shows that the separation of board chairman from CEO impacts negatively on the financial performance of Nigerian family owned firms. A priori, it is expected that concentrated ownership by providing better monitoring incentives should lead to better performance. However, some scholars and practitioner have argued that weak external governance mechanisms in less developed economies might give a powerful CEO the incentive to appropriate shareholders' fund for selfish end.

This study addresses one important question of whether or not, the emphasis of corporate codes in Nigeria should focus frontally on resolving agency conflict using the agency theory prescription. The findings reveal that while the separation of the position of CEO from board chair may be dependent on ownership structure, the focus should be on regulation that will foster strong external governance laws in Nigeria.

POLICY IMPLICATION

Institutional peculiarities in corporate governance arrangements in different countries have raised the advocacy for institutional perspective of agency theory in corporate governance research, especially, in developing economies. One of the striking differences between countries corporate governance systems is the ownership and control structures that exist among countries. While some systems are characterized by dispersed ownership structure, others tend to tilt towards concentrated ownership structure like family holding, bloc alliance, or financial institutions acting through a holding company (Maher and Andersson, 1999). These characteristics also influenced the nature of corporate governance problems found in those jurisdictions. The findings of this study reveal that the ownership structure argument should not be relegated to the shadows, especially in developing economies.

The effectiveness of corporate governance systems is influenced by product market competition, the structure of capital and labour markets, and the regulatory and legal framework. On the regulatory and legal framework, Shleifer and Vishny (1997) argue that much of the differences in corporate governance systems around the world stem from varying regulatory and legal environments.

In Nigeria, there is, near lack of basic infrastructures, corporate frauds, tax evasion, inexperience management, incessant changes in government macroeconomic and fiscal policies, communal and civil unrest, among others in Nigeria. Governments and host communities have ways of meddling with the affairs of firms. In some other cases, corporate owners and managers deliberately embark on acts that serve more of self than the overall wellbeing of the affected firms. Most board members perceive their role as mere advisory, and do not in any way strive to resolve the excess power of overbearing CEO whether there position of board chair is separated or not.

Policy recommendations should take into cognizance the peculiarity of Nigeria corporate environment. The search for good practice should be based on the identification of what works in Nigeria. Ultimately, the sustainability of reforms in Nigeria will depend on the institutional infrastructure within the country to enforce the rules on a consistent and fair basis, and a gradual but firm culture change.

Variable	**BDuality**	**LogTA**	**ROAE**	**LogAge**
BDuality	1.0000			
LogTA	-0.0176	1.0000		
ROAE	-0.0267	-0.1015	1.0000	
LogAge	0.0851	-0.1035	0.0095	1.000

*correlation is significant at the 0.05 level (2-tailed).

Source: Computed from Handpicked Data (Using Stata-Computa Analytical Package).

Figure 4. Correlation Matrix of Ownership Dispersed Firms.

```
. regress ROAE BDuality LogTA LogAge

      Source |       SS       df       MS              Number of obs =    1795
-------------+------------------------------           F(  3,  1791) =    3.05
       Model |  42.4175641     3  14.139188            Prob > F      =  0.0276
    Residual |  8301.87811  1791  4.63533116           R-squared     =  0.0051
-------------+------------------------------           Adj R-squared =  0.0034
       Total |  8344.29567  1794   4.6512239           Root MSE      =   2.153

------------------------------------------------------------------------------
        ROAE |      Coef.   Std. Err.      t    P>|t|     [95% Conf. Interval]
-------------+----------------------------------------------------------------
    BDuality |  -.1578114   .1022893    -1.54   0.123    -.3584303    .0428075
       LogTA |  -.1060291   .0478133    -2.22   0.027    -.1998048   -.0122534
      LogAge |   .3319436   .2088508     1.59   0.112    -.0776733    .7415605
       _cons |   .4515175   .3967606     1.14   0.255    -.3266448     1.22968
```

Source: Stata Analytical Software Computations.

Figure 5. Pooled Regression Results of Ownership Dispersed Firms.

Thus, the corporate governance infrastructure will have to be developed. This will include developing a strong cadre of directors, auditors, regulators, and other professionals who understand their roles and exercise their responsibilities within the system. It will require significant investment in training and recruiting of competent and ethical individuals, as well as enforcement of the rules in a timely and fair manner. It is also very urgent to rethink company laws in Nigeria, and devise a proactive compliance culture and enforcement mechanism.

. regress ROAE BDuality LogTA LogAge

Source	SS	df	MS
Model	23.3180163	3	7.77267209
Residual	4995.56709	625	7.99290735
Total	5018.88511	628	7.99185527

Number of obs =	629
F(3, 625) =	0.97
Prob > F =	0.4053
R-squared =	0.0046
Adj R-squared =	-0.0001
Root MSE =	2.8272

ROAE	Coef.	Std. Err.	t	P>|t|	[95% Conf.	Interval]
BDuality	-.1489808	.2643398	-0.56	0.573	-.6680825	.3701209
LogTA	-.1668431	.1046516	-1.59	0.111	-.3723544	.0386683
LogAge	.0557649	.3949295	0.14	0.888	-.7197846	.8313144
_cons	1.231439	.9199554	1.34	0.181	-.5751391	3.038017

Source: Stata Analytical Software Computations.

Figure 6. Pooled Regression Results of Ownership Concentrated Firms.

REFERENCES

Anderson, C.A. and Anthony, R.N. 1986. The New Corporate Directors, New York: John Wisely and Sons.

Berger, A. N. and Udell, G. F. 1998. The Economics of Small Business Finance: The Roles of Private Equity and Debt Markets in Financial Growth Cycle, *Journal of Banking & Finance,* 22(6-8), 613-673.

Booth, J. R., Cornett, M. M. and Tehranian, H. 2002. Board of Directors, Ownership, and Regulation", *Journal of Banking and Finance,* 26(1), 1973–1995.

Bosner, K. 2007. Board Composition, Structure, and Financial Performance: An Update", *Journal of Applied Business Researc*h, 23(4): 27-36.

Boyd, B. K. 1995.CEO Duality and Firm Performance: A Contingency Model, *Strategic Management Journal,* 16(4), 301–312.

Carter, D. A., Simkins, B. J. and Simpson, W. G. 2003.Corporate Governance, Board Diversity, and Firm Value" *Financial Review,* 38(1), 33–53.

Chancharat, N., Krishnamurti, C. and Tian, G. 2012. Board Structure and Survival of New Economy IPO Firm, Corporate Governance: An International Review, 20(2): 144-163.

Changanti, R.S., Mahajan, V. and Sharma, S. 1985. Corporate Board Size, Composition and Corporate Failures in Retailing Industry", *Journal of Management Studies*, 22(4): 400-417.

Charan, R. (1998). Boards at Work: How Corporate Boards Create Competitive Advantage. San Francisco, CA: Jossey-Bass Publishers.

Chen, W.C., Lin, B.J. and Yi. B. 2008. CEO Duality and Firm Performance: An Endogenous Issue", Corporate Ownership and Control, 6(1): 58-65.

Cochran, P. L. and Wood, R. A. 1984. Corporate Social Responsibility and Financial Performance. *Academy of Management Journal,* 27(1), 42–56.

Daily, C.M. and Dalton, D.R. 1994. Bankruptcy and Corporate Governance: The Impact of Board Composition and Structure", Entrepreneurship: *Theory and Practice,* 7(5): 375-386.

Dey, A., Engel, E. and Liu, X.G. 2009. Determinants and Implications of Board Leadership Structure", Retrieved 25th August, 2009 from http://ssrn.com/abstract=1412827.

Descender, K.A. 2009.The Relationship Between the Ownership Structure and the Role of the Board", University of Illinois Working Paper, Retrieved on 25th August, 2009 from http://www.business.illinois.edu/Working Papers/papers/09-0105.pdf.

Donaldson, L. and Davis, J.H. 1991.Stewardship Theory or Agency Theory: CEO Governance and Shareholder Returns", *Journal of Management,* 16(4): 49-64.

Erhardt, N. L; Werbel, J. D. and Shrader, C. B. 2003.Board of Director Diversity and Firm Performance" *Corporate Governance: An International Review,* 11(2), 102–111.

Fama, E. (1980), "Agency Problems and Theory of the Firm", *Journal of Political Economy*, 88: 288-307.

Fama, E. F. and Jensen, M. C. 1983. Separation of Ownership and Control" *Journal of Law and Economics,* 26(2), 301–325.

Fox, A.M. 1998. Board of Directors: The Influence of Board Size, Leadership and Composition on Corporate Financial Performance", *Commerce Division Discussion Papers* No.45: 1-15.

Gregory, B. T., Rutherford, M. W., Oswald, S. and Gardiner, L. 2005. An Empirical Investigation of the Growth Cycle Theory of Small Firm Financing. *Journal of Small Business Management,* 43(4), 382-392.

Hambrick, D.C. and D'Aveni, R.A. 1992. *Top Team Deterioration as Part of the Downward Spiral of Large Corporation Bankruptcies, Management Science,* 38(10): 1445-1466.

Jensen, M. and Meckling, W. 1976.Theory of the Firm, Managerial Behaviour, Agency Costs and Ownership Structure, *Journal of Financial Economics,* 3, 305-350.

Kiel, G. and Nicholson. G. 2003.Board Composition and Corporate Performance: How the Australian experience Informs Contrasting

Theories of Corporate Governance" *Corporate Governance: An International Review,* 11(3), 189–205.

Lipczinsky, J. and Wilson, J. 2001. Industrial Organisation: An Analysis of Competitive Markets. London: Prentice Hall.

Maher, M. and Andersson, T. 1999.Corporate Governance: Effects on Firm Performance and Economic Growth", OECD Working Paper: 1-51.

Muth, M. M. and Donaldson, L. 1998 Stewardship Theory and Board Structure: A Contingency Approach. *Corporate Governance: An International Review,* 6(1), 5-28.

Norman, M.S., Iskander, T.M. and Rahmat, M.M. 2005.Earnings Management and Board Characteristics: Evidence from Malaysia" *Journal Pengurusan,* 24: 77-103.

Peng, M.K., Zhang, S. and Li, X. 2007.CEO Duality and Firm Performance During China's Institutional Transitions", *Journal of Management and Organisational Review,* 3(2): 205-225.

Peasnell, K. V; Pope, P. F. andYoung, S. 2003.Managerial Equity Ownership and the Demand for Outside Directors. *European Financial Management,* 9(2), 231–250.

Pfeffer, J. 1972. Size and Composition of Corporate Boards of Directors: The Organization and its Environment. *Administrative Science Quarterly,* 17(2), 218–228.

Shleifer, A. and Vishny,R. 1997.A Survey of Corporate Governance", *Journal* of Finance, 52(2), pp. 737-783.

Shrader, C. B; Blackburn, V. B. and Illes, P. 1997.Women in Management and Firm Financial Value: An Exploratory Study" *Journal of Managerial Issues,* 9(3), 355–372.

Seifert, B. and Gonenc, H. 2012 Creditor Rights and R&D Expenditures, Corporate Governance: *An International Review,* 20(1): 3-20.

Singh, D.A. and Gaur, A.S. 2009.Business Group Affiliation, Firm Governance and Firm Performance: Evidence from China and India.

Sridharan, U.V. and Marsinko, A. 2007.CEO Duality in the Paper and Forest Products Industry", *Journal of Financial and Strategic Decision,* 10(1): 59-65.

Stewart, R. 1991.Chairman and Chief Executives: An Explanation of their Relationship" Journal of Management Studies, 28(5): 511-527.

Wooldridge, J. 2002. Econometric Analysis of Cross Section and Panel Data. Cambridge, MA: MIT Press.

Zahra, S. and Pearce, J. 1989.Board of Directors and Corporate Financial Performance: A Review and Integrated Model", *Journal of Management,* 15: 291-244.

Zajac, E. J.and Westphal, J. D. 1996.Director Reputation, CEO-Board Power, and the Dynamics of Board Interlocks". *Administrative Science Quarterly,* 41, 507–52.

Vaugirard, V. 2004.Clientelism, Debt Service and Governance", *Advances in Financial Economies,* 9: *137- 160.*

In: Financial Performance
Editor: Elaine Moreno
ISBN: 978-1-63484-501-4

Chapter 3

Corporate Governance Scores and Financial Performance: Do Revisions Matter?

Claude Francoeur[1,*], MBA, PhD, CPA, CGA, and Joseph Gawer[2,†], PhD

[1]HEC Montreal, Montreal, Quebec, Canada
[2]Université Paris Dauphine,
Place du Maréchal de Lattre de Tassigny,
NATIXIS Asset Management, Paris, France

Abstract

This study takes a closer look at how corporate governance practices are evaluated by stock market participants. The recent study of Bebchuck, Cohen, and Wang (2013) has documented the disappearance of the governance-return association that existed during the 1990s. According to these authors, market participants have learned to fully appreciate corporate governance scores. This paper revisits this question by specifically looking at the association between revisions in corporate governance (CG) scores and subsequent stock returns. We therefore focus on the improvement or deterioration of CG quality, rather than its

* Tel: 514-340-6847; email: claude.francoeur@hec.ca.
† Tel: 33 1 78 40 86 29, email: joseph.gawer@am.natixis.com.

absolute value, as a potential source of stock market anomaly. We use an event study methodology to measure the market reaction to changes in the CG scores of 600 European public companies between 1999 and 2009. The results show that firms experiencing downward revisions are associated with long-term underperformance and weak and stable tracking-error volatility. This suggests that CG negative revisions is a source of abnormal returns that could be harnessed by professional financial analysts.

Keywords: corporate governance, stock returns, long-term performance, financial analysts

I. INTRODUCTION

Do investors price corporate governance (CG) practices adequately? Gompers, Ishii, and Metrick (2003) find that, in the 1990s, US companies showing higher CG scores outperformed their peers with lower scores. But, during the 2000 decade, Bebchuk, Cohen and Wang (2012) find that this "market anomaly" had disappeared. The market had apparently learned how to correctly differentiate between good-governance and bad-governance firms when forecasting their expected future profitability.[1]

This study takes a closer look at this debate by evaluating the impact of CG revisions, rather than CG absolute values, on firm financial performance among 16 European countries. Results show that short selling the stocks of firms experiencing downward CG score revisions is a profitable strategy that bears moderate risk.

In recent years, corporate governance (CG) has received increased attention because of high-profile scandals involving the abuse of corporate power and, in some cases, criminal activity by corporate officers. The stock market crisis of 2000–2003 is known to be due in part to poor CG. Legislators and regulators tend to address this type of crisis by introducing reforms aimed at "restoring confidence" between investors and other stakeholders.

[1] One could argue that in view of the efficient market hypothesis, CG scores changes should readily be incorporated in stock prices. But, previous studies have showed that the stock market efficiency hypothesis only holds in its semi-strong form (e.g., Sloan, 1996, Xie, 2001). Gathering this type of information is costly and only slowly incorporates stock prices.

Many studies have found a *contemporaneous* correlation between firm performance[2] and the quality of CG (Gompers, Ishii, and Metrick (2003), Brown and Caylor (2009), Bebchuk, Cohen and Ferrell (2009)). The existing literature has found that CG score levels are contemporaneously correlated with firm performance. However, none of these studies focuses on investors' potential reaction to changes in CG scores. This paper attempts to address this gap in the literature by specifically examining the association between revisions in CG scores and subsequent firm returns. We do so by investigating the monthly CG scores provided by Vigeo, a respected European corporate social responsibility and CG ratings agency, while tracking the impact of a series of events—changes in CG scores—in the financial market.

We first calculate and test for statistical significance over a 24-month period the abnormal returns of equity portfolios built according to the sign of the revisions of the CG scores. Our event study is built on an event time approach and we use the specific statistical tests presented by Lyon, Barber, and Tsai (1999) to account for the effect of the skew distribution usually observed in long-term abnormal returns. We then examine the risks associated to the returns by focusing on the tracking error, that is, the standard deviation of the abnormal returns, of the two sub-samples of companies with revised CG scores.

Results indicate an absence of long-term over-performance or underperformance for upwardly revised companies. On the contrary, the portfolios of downwardly revised companies exhibit significant negative abnormal returns ranging from -4.7% after a 12-month period down to -8.9% after 24 months and low tracking-error volatility. We conclude that CG negative revisions could be a source a potential gains for professional financial analysts using a short-sell strategy.

The remainder of this paper is organized as follows: The next section briefly overviews the financial literature on the relation between CG and firm performance. Section III describes our hypotheses. Section IV describes our sample and data sources. Section V presents the methodology. Section VI presents the results of our empirical investigations on the relations between CG, stock returns, and risk. The final section concludes with a summary and offers suggestions for future research.

---

[2] For a discussion of the measurement of firm performance and corporate governance, see Charreaux and Desbrières (1998).

II. LITERATURE REVIEW

Previous studies on the link between firm performance and CG broadly distinguish three types of results concerning the sign of the relation: positive, negative, and neutral. The seminal paper of Gompers, Ishii, and Metrick (2003) presents evidence of a positive association between CG and long-term stock returns, firm value, and accounting measures of performance. The authors use 24 measures of CG provided by the Investor Responsibility Research Center (IRRC) for 1,500 US firms from 1990–1999 to test their impact on financial performance. The authors construct a governance index to proxy for the level of shareholders rights, an aggregate measure of CG. They construct portfolios consisting of firms with numerous anti-takeover amendments ("dictatorship portfolios") and portfolios including firms with very few amendments ("democracy portfolios"). They then examine the returns to holding a long position in the democracy portfolio and a short position in the dictatorship portfolio. This long-short strategy yields average returns of 8.5% per year. This study also shows that well-governed companies are valued higher by the market and their accounting statements show better operating performance.[3] These results clearly support the hypothesis that well-governed companies outperform their poorly governed counterparts.

Drobetz, Schillhofer, and Zimmermann (2004) analyze the impact of CG on stock returns over the period 1998–2002 in Germany. Due to the fact that their CG data are limited to one observation, March 2002, they assume constant historical ratings. To construct their sample, the authors sent out questionnaires to 253 German firms in different market segments and received answers from about 36% of these firms. In line with Gompers, Ishii, and Metrick (2003), they compare two portfolios consisting of well-governed versus poorly governed firms. Their results show an annual excess return of close to 12% in favor of well-governed firms.

Klapper and Love (2004) analyze the association between CG and firm performance in emerging markets. They use data on firm-level CG rankings across 14 countries in 1999, on a sample of 335 firms. They find that companies with better governance and better disclosure standards exhibit higher Tobin's Q values.

[3] The valuation is proxied by Tobin's Q and the operational measures are the net profit margin, return on equity, and one-year sales growth. Tobin's Q is defined as the market value of assets (calculated as the book value of assets minus the book value of equity plus the market value of equity) over the book value of assets.

Core, Guay, and Rusticus (2006) examine the relation between CG and financial performance. Like Gompers, Ishii, and Metrick (2003), they use 24 measures of CG provided by the IRRC on US firms from 1990 to 1999 and analyze their financial impacts. They find evidence that weak shareholder rights are associated with lower operating performance as proxied by return on assets (ROA).

Beiner, Drobetz, Schmid, and Zimmermann (2006) analyze the impact of CG on firm valuation in 2003 in Switzerland. They construct a CG index based on the recommendations and suggestions of the Swiss Code of Best Practice. They examine a sample of 109 Swiss firms and find a positive relation between the CG index and Tobin's Q.

Philippon (2006) provides empirical evidence that badly governed firms have lower profit margins and more cyclical sales than well-governed firms. The author builds a model where managers are prone to over-invest and shareholders are more likely to tolerate such behavior when times are good. Managerial tendencies to increase investment, employment, and output—together with the proposition that shareholders leave more discretion to managers in good times—implies that CG conflicts between managers who tend to expand their firms beyond the profit-maximizing size and shareholders amplify the fluctuations of those business cycle indicators.

Bhagat and Bolton (2008) consider seven different governance measures. They find that better corporate governance, board members' stock ownership and CEO-Chair separation are significantly positively associated with better contemporaneous and subsequent operating performance. But interestingly, they find that board independence is negatively correlated with contemporaneous and subsequent operating performance.

Clacher, Doriye, and Hillier (2008) study 63 UK firms of the FTSE 100 over the period 2003–2005. They find that the well-governed companies are associated with higher Tobin's Q and ROA, as well as lower levels of capital expenditure. The authors explain that stronger governance structures implicitly reduce the ability of executives to over-invest in projects that do not maximize shareholder wealth.

Aggarwal, Erel, Stulz, and Williamson (2008) use data from RiskMetrics (formerly Institutional Shareholder Service, or ISS[4]) and compare the governance of non-US firms with a matched set of US firms and find that the valuation of non-US firms falls as their governance index value decreases

[4] In 2005, Institutional Shareholder Services (ISS) acquired Investor Responsibility Research Center (IRRC). In 2007 RiskMetrics acquired ISS.

compared to the governance index of matching US firms. Specifically, the authors find strong evidence that non-US firms invest less in internal governance mechanisms that increase the power of minority shareholders than comparable US firms do.

Chhaochharia and Laeven (2009) evaluate the impact of firm-level CG provisions on the valuation of 2,300 firms in 23 developed countries for the period 2003–2005. They use CG data from the ISS database and find a positive association between CG and firm valuation. Despite the cost associated with improving CG, a one standard deviation increase in the difference between firm-level governance scores and the minimally accepted country-level governance is associated with an 8% increase in Tobin's Q.

Cheung, Jiang, Limpaphayom, and Lu (2010) examine the relation between the quality of CG practices and the market valuation of Chinese listed firms and develop a CG index based on the Organisation for Economic Co-operation and Development's (OECD) Principle of Corporate Governance (OECD, 2004). Their sample consists of the 100 largest Chinese listed companies over the period 2004–2006. They find a positive relation between CG practices and market valuation.

Cheung, Connelly, Jiang, and Limpaphayom (2011) examine how changes in the quality of CG practices relate to changes in subsequent market valuation for Hong Kong listed companies. To assess the quality of CG practices, the authors create their own CG index based on a CG scoring method derived from CG principles (OECD, 2004). They construct a database of CG data for the years 2002, 2004, and 2005 from the Hong Kong Institute of Directors. Using a sample of 510 firm–year observations, they find a positive correlation between changes in the quality of CG practices and subsequent changes in market valuation, as measured by Tobin's Q or the market-to-book ratio.

Bauer, Günster, and Otten (2004) find a negative association between CG and financial performance. The authors use the Deminor Corporate Governance ratings for European Monetary Union (EMU) and UK companies included in the FTSE Eurotop 300 index. Assuming constant historical ratings, as Drobetz, Schillhofer, and Zimmermann (2004), they find a negative correlation between CG and firm performance proxied by net profit margin and return on equity (ROE).

Bebchuk, Cohen, and Ferrell (2009) examine which provisions matter among the 24 provisions of the IRRC in the relation between CG and financial performance. They identify six entrenching provisions that are negatively correlated with firm performance proxied by Tobin's Q, as well as stock returns, over the period 1990–2003 in the United States.

Finally, certain studies offer mixed results about the relation between CG and financial performance. Brown and Caylor (2006) build a governance index that includes 51 governance factors provided by the ISS in 2003. Their study show that corporations with low CG scores generally exhibit lower ROA and ROE. Among the 51 ISS provisions, they identify only 10 factors that show positive correlations with at least one of the two performance measures.

Bassen, Prigge, and Zöllner (2008) examine the impact of CG in Germany by using the individual provisions of the German Corporate Governance Code (GCGC). The authors find that for a sample of 100 large companies, compliance with GCGC is globally negatively associated with Tobin's Q. A more in-depth analysis reveals that three specific GCGC recommendations are not associated with financial performance measures, while four others are negatively associated.

Johnson, Moorman, and Sorescu (2009) re-examine the long-term abnormal return findings of Gompers, Ishii, and Metrick (2003) and find that firms in democracy and dictatorship portfolios are distributed differently across industries. They argue that the presence of industry clustering raises concerns about the robustness of the abnormal returns observed by Gompers, Ishii, and Metrick (2003). Using a finer three-digit Standard Industrial Classification (SIC) code industry return adjustment, Johnson, Moorman, and Sorescu (2009) find no significant differences between long-term abnormal returns between these portfolios.

Bebchuck, Cohen, and Wang (2013) also re-examine the trading strategy based on an index of 24 governance provisions from Gompers, Ishii, and Metrick (2003). Their data consists of all companies included in the eight volumes published by the Investor Responsibility Research Center (IRRC) from 1990 to 2006. They do not use the data in the 2008 RiskMetrics governance volume because it is not comparable with data in the earlier IRRC volumes. Indeed, in 2007, RiskMetrics acquired ISS and revamped its data collection methods. Consequently, changes were made in the set of provisions covered and in the definitions of some of these provisions. Bebchuck, Cohen, and Wang (2013) present evidence to suggest that the positive long-run returns on the Gompers, Ishii, and Metrick (2003) long-short governance portfolios were specific to the period 1991-1999. Nevertheless, they show that this same strategy was no longer associated with abnormal returns during the period 2000-2008. They find that subsequent disappearance of the abnormal return on this portfolio cannot be fully explained either by additional common risk factors suggested in the literature for augmenting the Fama-French-Carhart four-factor model. They suggest that the disappearance of the governance-returns association in the 2000s was due to market participants' learning to appreciate the difference between firms scoring well and poorly on the governance indices.

Using the Vigeo ratings over the period 2003-2010, Girerd-Potin, Jimenez-Garcès and Louvet (2014) explore the link between stock returns and three socially responsible dimensions: business stakeholders, societal stakeholders and financial stakeholders. They show that investors ask for an additional risk premium when they accept to hold non-socially responsible stocks.

A stream of literature argues that analysts provide information that is not yet incorporated into market prices. Revisions concerning financial forecasts have then interest to investors since then reveal a change in analyst opinion. Green (2006) and Chang and Chan (2008) highlight that these revisions can be useful for active portfolio management. For Gleason and Lee (2003) market adjusts slowly to information coming from revisions of earnings estimates made by the analysts, and subsequent revisions behave as catalysts in the formation of share prices. By exploiting the information contained in the CG scores made by analysts, we seek to understand how CG scores revisions participate in the formation of stock prices.

III. Hypothesis Development

This study investigates revisions in CG performance in Europe, using a sample of 600 firms covered by the Vigeo organization during a 10-year period from 1999 to 2009. Upward and downward revisions are measured as year-to-year differences. We first compare two portfolios of upward and downward CG revisions for differences between the stock returns of the revised companies and the returns of the benchmark over the post-revision period and test the following hypotheses.

H1a: In the post-revision period, long-term abnormal returns for portfolios of upward CG revisions are null; that is, there is no difference between the returns of the portfolio of upwardly revised companies and those of the benchmark.

H1b: In the post-revision period, long-term abnormal returns for portfolios of downward CG revisions are null; that is, there is no difference between the returns of the portfolio of downwardly revised companies and those of the benchmark.

Rejecting these hypotheses would suggest that the market does not incorporate CG score revisions in stock returns in a timely manner. Post-revision abnormal performance could result from risk factors that are unknown to capital market analysts.

As a robustness check, we test for any abnormal performance of the CG-revised companies prior to the revisions. Finding abnormal prior to CG revisions could suggest that the stock market is able to anticipate the impact of the revisions in CG scores susceptible to being reflected in stock returns.

H2a: In the pre-revision period, long-term abnormal returns for portfolios of upward CG revisions are null; that is, there is no difference between the returns of the portfolio of upwardly revised companies and those of the benchmark.

H2b: In the pre-revision period, long-term abnormal returns for portfolios of CG downward revisions are null; that is, there is no difference between the returns of the portfolio of downwardly revised companies and those of the benchmark.

Evidence of statistically significant abnormal returns between the upwardly and downwardly revised companies can suggest the presence of information asymmetry triggering different behaviors from the market, given good or bad news conveyed by the information associated with the revisions.

Finally, an analysis of the tracking-error volatility over the post-revision period could indicate whether the impact of CG score revisions on share price causes a deviation of the risk relative to the benchmark.

IV. METHODOLOGY

Firm-Level Data on CG Scores and Returns

One important source of source for CG scores for European companies is the Vigeo database. Vigeo is a major European supplier of extra-financial analysis that assesses the degree to which companies take into account environmental, social, societal, and CG objectives. Vigeo values six dimensions: human resources, environment, corporate governance, community involvement, business behavior, and human rights (see Appendix 1). The dimensions covered are similar to the ones used by Our goal in the USA.

Cellier and Chollet (2012) gives a detailed comparison between KLD and Vigeo methodologies.

One previous study on Vigeo scores is the Cellier and Chollet (2011) event study. They measure the impact of Vigeo corporate social rating announcements from 2004 to 2009 on short term stock returns on the European stock market. They find a positive significant influence of the CG announcement on stock returns over two days prior to the announcement and two days following.

Our work extends that of Cellier and Chollet (2012). We are also exploring the impact of CG scores on equity returns from the Vigeo database. However, three features of our research differ from their work. Their paper examines the relationship between the CG scores and returns on short investment periods. Our research examines the medium-term impact of CG scores on 24 investment horizons from 1 to 24 months after the announcement of the score. We focus between positive or negative changes of CG scores rather than static values. Finally, we consider the accumulation of positive or negative CG score changes as a stronger signal of the improvement or degradation of the firm governance practices.

Vigeo publishes firm-specific CG scores that aggregate[5] the scores on four sub-criteria of CG: the board of directors, audit and internal controls, shareholders, and executive remuneration.[6] The scores are revised during sector reviews that usually take place annually. However, Vigeo's analysts can change the score of a company at any time through alerts. In general, Vigeo's scores are updated yearly. They aim at measuring the quality of CG, that is, the adoption of more or less good governance practices. Vigeo CG scores have been often used by academics and practitioners to study the relation between the CG and financial performance.

Vigeo covers European stocks belonging to the European Dow Jones Stoxx 600 index. This index includes large, mid, and small capitalization companies across 18 countries of the European region: Austria, Belgium, Denmark, Finland, France, Germany, Greece, Iceland, Ireland, Italy, Luxembourg, the Netherlands, Norway, Portugal, Spain, Sweden, Switzerland, and the United Kingdom.

Our basic sample comprises all 600 European firms included in the Dow Jones Stoxx 600 index as of March 31, 2009. To avoid any new listing and

[5] The weighting of the criteria that make up the aggregate Vigeo CG score is proprietary information.

[6] See the Appendix 1 for Vigeo's definitions of the four criteria.

survivor bias, we excluded from the initial sample all firms that began or stopped trading subsequent to a CG score revision.

Vigeo's historical database for European firms starts in 1999. Our sample of Vigeo's scores is a panel with 36,281 firm–month CG scores data over the period December 31, 1999, to March 31, 2009. Table 1 reports the percentage of firms with Vigeo CG scores. At the end of 2003 more than half of the companies were scored on CG by Vigeo. At the end of March 2009, 86% of the 600 companies were scored. These 517 firms account for over 97% of the total market capitalization of the Dow Jones Stoxx 600 index of March 31, 2009.

Table 2 and 3 show yearly corporate governance average scores by country and industrial sector respectively. On average, northern european countries such as UK, Ireland, Finland and The Netherlands tend to score higher than southern ones, e.g., Italy, Portugal and Greece. In contrast, no industrial sector seem to dominate or underperform during the period observed.

Table 1. Percentage of Dow Jones Stoxx 600 firms covered by Vigeo

Date	Percentage of firms with CG scores
12/31/1999	20%
12/31/2000	27%
12/31/2001	33%
12/31/2002	38%
12/31/2003	56%
12/31/2004	60%
12/31/2005	64%
12/31/2006	67%
12/31/2007	74%
12/31/2008	82%
03/31/2009	86%

This table reports the percentage of firms with CG scores for each year from 1999 to 2009, provided by Vigeo, among the 600 European firms included in the Dow Jones Stoxx 600 index as of March 31, 2009.

Table 2. Corporate Governance average scores per Country and per Year

Country Average Score	1999	2000	2001	2002	2003	2004	2005	2006	2007	2008	2009
Austria			46	43	43	43	41	40	40	42	41
Belgium	35	35	50	51	50	47	36	34	37	35	36
Denmark			58	58	45	41	31	33	33	28	28
Finland	48	64	55	57	56	48	43	45	52	49	48
France	55	47	59	56	52	46	40	41	40	40	42
Germany	41	46	54	52	51	48	41	42	42	41	41
Greece				38	34	32	23	22	24	27	28
Ireland	60	60	73	65	59	56	54	48	47	50	50
Italy	23	14	43	43	44	41	33	33	34	35	36
Netherlands	47	56	63	60	52	48	49	53	57	57	60
Norway						44	38	48	54	53	54
Portugal	30	16	41	40	42	32	28	32	33	33	33
Spain	30	22	51	48	47	43	39	42	41	38	39
Sweden				47	46	42	39	41	41	40	40
Switzerland			44	43	49	50	43	42	42	42	42
United Kingdom				57	56	56	61	63	65	66	66
Total	41	40	53	50	48	45	40	41	43	42	43

Table 3. Corporate Governance average scores per Sector and per Year

Sector Average Score	1999	2000	2001	2002	2003	2004	2005	2006	2007	2008	2009
Consumer Discretionary	46	45	60	55	52	45	38	38	40	40	42
Consumer Staples	58	49	57	58	53	46	38	37	38	38	38
Energy	54	55	58	61	54	43	43	45	39	39	42
Financials	76	55	58	58	54	50	47	45	43	46	46
Health Care	0	39	66	66	57	54	36	36	41	43	39
Industrials	58	46	58	54	48	46	37	36	36	35	36
Information Technology	52	40	55	50	49	41	40	50	47	44	49
Materials	67	45	69	65	65	48	46	48	43	42	47
Telecommunication Services	53	52	49	50	50	31	41	41	42	42	41
Utilities				50	50	47	64	46	41	46	45
Total	58	47	59	57	53	45	43	42	41	41	42

We use the FactSet historical databases to measure financial performance. In contrast to previous studies, we study the CG score's *revision* rather than their level to test the relation between CG and stock returns. Some studies have shown that *levels* in CG scores are contemporaneously correlated with firm performance. However, none of these studies focuses on the investors' potential reaction in the capital market associated with the *changes* in the CG scores. This study argues that an indicator of CG *revision*, which measures the improvement or, conversely, the degradation of governance practices within a company, is more appropriate to detect any potential impact on financial performance.

The revision is calculated as the difference between two consecutive CG scores:

$$\text{Rev}_{i,t} = \text{Score}_{i,t} - \text{Score}_{i,t-1}$$

where $\text{Score}_{i,t}$ is the level of the CG score on security *i* in month *t* and the CG scores are between zero and 100.

Positive (negative) $\text{Rev}_{i,t}$ values are classified as upward (downward) revisions. For each sub-sample, namely, the upward and downward revision samples, we determine the future abnormal returns and test for their statistical significance.

What Type of Revision to Choose to Examine Market Impact?

Our goal is to understand the strengthening of the conviction of the rating agency on the improvement or degradation of firm governance practices. We believe that the accumulation of positive or negative revisions on the governance of a firm CG is a tool to measure the evolution of the firm's governance practices. The more positive revisions rise (fall), the more the rating agency believes that the company's governance practices improve (deteriorate). The conviction of the improvement (deterioration) of CG practices is even more pronounced if it results from a continuous stream of positive (negative) revisions. Conversely, an alternation of the sign of revisions reflects the uncertainty of the rating agency on governance practices of the firm.

However, should we consider only the returns of firms that have recorded consecutive revisions in the same direction? This request of continuity in the sign of revisions would lead to select the firms to which the agency has only strengthened its conviction. In reality, 5 or 6 revisions of the same sign in a row are exceptional. Indeed, according to the Vigeo methodology the scores are between 0 and 100. Therefore, the probability of continuity in the sign of revisions decreases as the number of revisions increases, particularly when scores are close to these boundaries.

To avoid locking ourselves into an overly restrictive approach, we relax our request of continuity in the sign of revisions joining the possibility of an alternation of sign within a set of revisions. That is why we hold the firms that were revised in the same direction "at least" a number of times. For example, firms those have been negatively revised at least 4 times and were able to record 3 consecutive negative revisions then a positive revision and finally a negative revision. Finally, it is from the date of the fourth negative revision that we measure subsequent returns.

Table 4. Multiple revisions of CG scores statistics

Number of Revisions (X)	Number of CG scores revised upward at least X times	Number of CG scores revised downward at least X times
1	822	731
2	304	255
3	**132**	**120**
4	52	46
5	11	14
6	0	1

This table reports statistics on the number of upward and downward revisions in CG scores by equity from 1999 to 2009 among the 600 European firms included in the Dow Jones Stoxx 600 index as of March 31, 2009. The figure at the intersection of the first row and second column shows that 822 CG scores were upwardly revised at least one time. The figure at the intersection of the third row and second column shows that 132 CG scores were revised upward at least three times. The figure at the intersection of the third row and third column shows that 120 CG scores were revised downward at least three times.

We examine subsequent returns after a certain number of revisions in the same direction. We hold six thresholds of cumulative revisions. We first measure the subsequent returns after at least 6 negative revisions. Table 4 shows that only one firm reached this threshold. Then we measure the subsequent returns after at least five negative revisions and so on until we reach the level of at least a single negative revision (N = 731). Symmetrically, we also measure subsequent returns at six thresholds of cumulative positive revisions.

Long-Term Abnormal Returns

The literature about methodologies used to measure long-term abnormal returns has grown substantially in the past few years (Barber and Lyon (1997), Kothari and Warner (1997), Lyon, Barber, and Tsai (1999), Mitchell and Stafford (2000)). There are basically two methods to calculate long-term abnormal returns: via cumulative abnormal returns (CARs) and via buy-and-hold abnormal returns (BHARs). Barber and Lyon (1997) and Lyon, Barber, and Tsai (1999) find that CARs are biased estimators of long-run abnormal returns and favor the use of BHARs in tests designed to detect long-run abnormal stock returns. Kothari and Warner (1997) also recommended BHARs since the cumulating procedures in CARs lead to systematically positively biased abnormal returns. Other studies, however, favor the use of CARs over BHARs. Fama (1998) and Mitchell and Stafford (2000) advocate the CAR method in conjunction with the *calendar time* portfolio approach. However, Gompers and Lerner (2003) advise that the choice between the two approaches should largely depend on the implicit trading strategy that is being assumed. Therefore, a BHAR approach is deemed appropriate to this study to avoid the problems associated with frequent transactions and to facilitate a measure of differential returns on equivalent risk assets.

The BHAR Method

The BHAR is defined as the return on buy-and-hold investment in a firm less the return on a buy-and-hold investment in an asset/portfolio with an appropriate expected return. The BHARs $BHAR_{i,k}$ is obtained by subtracting the expected compounded returns for security i from its actual compounded returns over a k-month holding period following the event:

$$BHAR_{i,k} = \prod_{t=1}^{k}\left(1 + r_{i,t}\right) - \prod_{t=1}^{k}\left(1 + E\left[r_{i,t}\right]\right) \quad (1)$$

This method allows checking whether the mean abnormal return after the event period is different from zero. "The advantage of this approach is that it yields an abnormal return measure that accurately represents investor experience" (Lyon, Barber, and Tsai (1999), p. 198).

Evaluation of Long-Term Abnormal Returns

There are mainly two valuation methods for assessing long-term abnormal returns: the reference portfolio and the control firm methods. Generally, these use the size and book-to-market ratio (book value over market value) to compare sample firms to peer companies bearing similar risks. The use of these factors as firm risk measures results from the work of Fama and French (1992, 1993). Barber and Lyon (1997) and Kothari and Warner (1997) advocate the use of a single control firm as a benchmark because reference portfolios introduce new listing, rebalancing, and skewness biases in the calculation of BHARs. However, Lyon, Barber, and Tsai (1999) point out that carefully constructed reference portfolios, as in this study, overcome these sources of bias and smooth out the measurement noise related to the use of a single control firm. Hence, we use the reference portfolio as a proxy for the expected holding period return in Equation (1).

Reference Portfolio

We first compound the returns on securities that constitute the reference portfolio:

$$r_{psk}^{bh} = \sum_{i=1}^{n_s} \frac{\left[\prod_{t=s}^{s+k}\left(1 + r_{it}\right)\right] - 1}{n_s} \quad (2)$$

where s is the beginning period, k is the period of investment (in months), r_{it} is the return on security i in month t, and n_s is the number of securities traded in month s. The return on this portfolio represents a passive equally weighted investment in all securities constituting the reference portfolio in period s. There is no investment in firms newly listed subsequent to period s, nor is there monthly rebalancing of the portfolio. Consequently, in reference to the buy-and-hold nature of this return calculation, we denote the return calculated in this manner with the superscript *bh*.

The abnormal return calculation consists in comparing the returns of two portfolios *p* and *rp*. Portfolio p is our sample portfolio. Portfolio *rp*, the reference portfolio, groups equities that are not influenced by the event and which are similar to those of portfolio *p* in terms of size and book-to-market ratio. Following this method, the abnormal return $AR_{i,t}$ is defined as the difference between the actual month *t* return $r_{i,t}$ for security *i* and its month *t* reference portfolio return $r_{rpi,t}$:

$$AR_{i,t} = r_{i,t} - r_{rpi,t} \tag{3}$$

The buy-and-hold returns for a revised CG score company *i* ($BHR_{i,k}$) are obtained by compounding its monthly returns over the *k*-month period following the month of the revision. This measure replicates an investment strategy that consists of buying and holding shares for a period of time. The same logic applies to the reference portfolio *rp* associated with the revised firm *i*. The difference between the buy-and-hold return of the revised firm *i* and that of its reference portfolio *rpi* corresponds to the buy-and-hold abnormal return $BHAR_{i,k}$ for firm *i* over the *k*-month period:

$$BHR_{i,k} = \prod_{t=1}^{k} \left[\left(1 + r_{i,t} \right) \right] \tag{4}$$

$$BHAR_{i,k} = \prod_{t=1}^{k} \left(1 + r_{i,t} \right) - \prod_{t=1}^{k} \left(1 + r_{rpi,t} \right) \tag{5}$$

Consequently, the average BHARs (ABHARs) for *N* securities and for the *k*-month period following the event is the equal-weighted average of the BHARs of the individual stocks and is estimated as

$$ABHAR_{N,k} = \frac{1}{N}\sum_{i=1}^{N} BHAR_{i,k} \tag{6}$$

We examine the association between revisions in CG scores and subsequent firm returns, by splitting the sample of firms into two groups according to changes in their CG scores: those who experienced upward revisions in CG scores and those who experienced downward revisions. Using an event study approach, we measure the stock market reaction to revisions of CG scores during the period 1999–2009. To calculate abnormal returns we determine a reference portfolio for every stock. This approach enables us to account for the presence of stock market biases like size, valuation or price momentum effects.

Reference Portfolio Construction

We construct two families of reference portfolios: size over book to market portfolios and size over momentum return portfolios[7]. Following the works of Fama and French (1993) and Carhart (1997), our reference portfolios are formed on the basis of firm size and book-to-market ratios in July of each year, from 1997 through 2009. In addition, the second family of reference portfolios is formed on the basis of firm size and momentum return each month from March 31, 1999, to November 30, 2009.

Specifically, for each event firm (i.e., a company with a revised CG score), we compute its size and book-to-market ratio. We construct a reference portfolio, using a number of non-event (i.e., non-revised) firms chosen such that they are as similar as possible to each event firm in terms of size and book-to-market ratio. Identically, for each event firm, we compute its size and momentum return. We construct a reference portfolio using a number of non-event (i.e., non-revised) firms chosen such that they are as similar as possible to each event firm in terms of size and momentum return. We sort the firms

[7] For the sake of conciseness, we only provide the results for size over book-to-market portfolios.

according to their size, book-to-market ratio, and momentum return for each month over the sample period.

We construct two size reference portfolios as follows:

1. We take the free float market capitalization calculated by the Dow Jones in June of each year for all firms. The free float market capitalization is the portion of a stock's total market capitalization that is available for trading.
2. We sort stocks into two size groups: small stocks with June market capitalization below the median and big stocks with market cap above the median.

We construct three book-to-market ratio reference portfolios as follows:

1. We take the ratio of price to book calculated by Worldscope for all firms. The price-to-book ratio is the price in December of year t - 1 divided by the book value per share in year t - 1.
2. In December of year t - 1, we sort stocks into three book-to-market ratio (B/M) groups: growth stocks, in the bottom 30% of book-to-market ratios; neutral, with the middle 40% of book-to-market ratios; and value, in the top 30% of book-to-market ratios.

We construct three momentum return reference portfolios as follows.

The three momentum return reference portfolios are defined in the same manner as the three book-to-market ratio reference portfolios except that we sort on prior return rather than book-to-market ratio and the momentum sort is refreshed monthly rather than annually:

1. We take the momentum return (PR1Yr) for all firms. At the end of each month t - 1 we sort stocks on the 11 months of returns to the end of month t - 2. (Dropping the return for month t - 1 is common in the momentum literature).
2. Each month, we sort stocks into momentum return (PR1Yr) groups: low-momentum stocks in the bottom 30% of PR1Yr values; neutral, with the middle 40% of PR1Yr values; and high momentum, in the top 30% of PR1Yr values.

The intersection of the (independent) size and book-to-market ratio sorts produces six equally weighted portfolios refreshed at the end of June each year. In parallel, the intersection of the (independent) size and momentum return sorts produces six equally weighted portfolios refreshed monthly.

In conclusion, we construct two families of six reference portfolios: six size over book-to-market buy-and-hold portfolios and six size over momentum return buy-and-hold portfolios. We use these two families separately to compare the sample firms to peer companies bearing similar risks.

Statistical Tests

To address the previously highlighted problem of a positive skewness bias associated with the use of the BHAR methodology (Barber and Lyon (1997), Kothari and Warner (1997)), Lyon, Barber, and Tsai (1999) advocate the use of the skewness-adjusted t-statistic t_{sa}, suggested by Johnson (1978), to test the null hypothesis of abnormal returns to mitigate the skewness bias issue. This statistic adjusts the usual t-statistic by two terms that are a function of the skewness of the distribution of abnormal returns. Following this approach, the t_{sa} values for all $ABHAR_{N,k}$ are estimated as

$$t_{sa} = \sqrt{n}\left(S + \frac{1}{3}\hat{\gamma} S^2 + \frac{1}{6n}\hat{\gamma} \right) \tag{7}$$

where

$$S = \frac{\overline{ABHAR}}{\sigma\left(ABHAR\right)} \quad \text{and} \quad \hat{\gamma} = \frac{\sum_{i=1}^{n}\left(ABHAR_{N,k} - \overline{ABHAR}\right)^3}{n\,\sigma\left(ABHAR\right)^3}$$

Note that $\hat{\gamma}$ is an estimate of the coefficient of skewness.

Risk Examination

After having measured the abnormal performance of our sample, we examine the risks associated with the returns by focusing on the tracking-error volatility (TEV). The buy-and-hold strategy is a passive one, but, as mentioned by Grinold and Kahn (1989, p. 65), “passive managers want minimum tracking error.”

The tracking-error volatility measures how closely a sample follows the reference portfolio against which it is benchmarked. Roll (1992) notes that minimization of the tracking-error volatility has become an important criterion for assessing overall manager performance and Pope and Yadav (1994) agree that tracking errors are crucial to consider in structuring and managing portfolios.

As defined by Chincarini and Daehwan (2006), the tracking-error volatility is calculated as the standard deviation of the difference in returns between the portfolio and the benchmark. The tracking-error volatility for portfolio *pt* is estimated as

$$TEV = \sigma\left(R_{p,t} - R_{b,t}\right) = \sqrt{\frac{\sum_{t=1}^{n}\left(R_{p,t} - R_{b,t}\right)^2}{n}} \quad (8)$$

where *TEV* is the tracking-error volatility calculated from the monthly returns of the sub-sample *p,t* at month *t* and from the monthly returns of the benchmark *b,t* at month *t,* with *n* the number of months retained in the calculation of the standard deviation.

V. Empirical Results

Prior studies suggest that CG is strongly determined by country-specific factors. Bauer, Günster, and Otten (2003) find large differences in CG ratings across countries. Klapper and Love (2004) also show that firms’ CG practices are associated with country-level characteristics. According to Doidge, Karolyi, and Stulz (2007), country characteristics explain much more of the variance in CG ratings than observable firms’ characteristics.

If the weight of the countries most represented in the two sub-samples of revised CG score companies is different from the weight of the countries most represented in the benchmark portfolio, then the abnormal returns of the sub-samples could be explained by the presence of country bias. To control for this type of sample selection bias, we measure the percentage of equity by countries.

The number of listed firms per country and the weights of each country's equity value in the Dow Jones Stoxx 600 index and in the two sub-samples of revised CG scores are shown in Table 5. The second column of Table 5 presents the weight of each country in our equally weighted benchmark of Dow Jones Stoxx 600 companies. The third (fourth) column lists the weight of each country among the upwardly (downwardly) revised companies.

Table 5. Overview of the weights of firms with at least three revisions by country

Country	Numebr of firms listed in DJ Stoxx 600	Listed firms in DJ Stoxx 600 (%)	Density of listed firms in DJ Stoxx 600 (%)	Equities revised Upwards (%)	Equities revised Downwards (%)
United Kingdom	165	28%	28%	18%	0%
France	83	14%	41%	33%	43%
Germany	59	10%	51%	18%	17%
Switzerland	48	8%	59%	1%	3%
Italy	36	6%	65%	6%	12%
Spain	36	6%	71%	6%	6%
Sweden	35	6%	77%	0%	0%
Netherlands	27	5%	82%	11%	8%
Finland	19	3%	85%	2%	3%
Belgium	18	3%	88%	2%	4%
Denmark	18	3%	91%	0%	0%
Norway	14	2%	93%	2%	0%
Austria	12	2%	95%	0%	0%
Greece	11	2%	97%	0%	0%
Portugal	11	2%	99%	2%	2%
Ireland	8	1%	100%	2%	4%
Total	600	100%	100%	100%	100%

This table reports the weights of each country in the Dow Jones Stoxx 600 index as of March 31, 2009, and in the two sub-samples of companies with CG scores revised at least three times among the 600 selected European firms included in the Dow Jones Stoxx 600 index as of March 31, 2009. For instance, 165 UK firms were listed in the Dow Jones Stoxx 600 index as of March 31, 2009. This represents 28% of the equities of the equally weighted index. The figures at the intersection of the first row and the fifth and sixth column show that 18% of the UK firms were revised upward at least three times while 0% of the UK firms was revised downward at least three times over the period 1999-2009.

Table 6. Financial Characteristics of firms with at least three revisions of CG scores

Financial Caracteristics		Equities revised Upwards	%	Equities revised Downwards	%
Size	***Small***	23	17%	29	24%
	Big	108	**82%**	91	**76%**
Book/Market	***High***	40	30%	37	31%
	Med	61	46%	51	43%
	Low	29	22%	30	25%
Total of revisions		132		120	

This table reports the financial characteristics in terms of market capitalization and Book-to-market ratio of companies with CG scores revised at least three times among the 600 European firms included in the Dow Jones Stoxx 600 index as of March 31, 2009. For instance, over the period 1999-2009, among the 132 equities revised upwards, 108 of them – aka 82% – are big market cap firms. Among the 120 equities revised downwards, 91 of them – aka 76% – are also big market cap firms.

As of March 2009, the six countries most represented in the Stoxx 600 European equity index both in terms of number of companies and market capitalization are UK, France, Germany, Switzerland, Italy and Spain. Table 5 (4th column) shows these countries represent 71% of the index, namely 427 out of 600 companies. However, as seen in the fifth (sixth) column they represent 82% (81%) of the companies who have seen their CG scores revised upward (downward) at least three times.

Table 6 reports the financial characteristics in terms of market capitalization and Book-to-market ratio of companies with CG scores revised at least three times. CG scores revisions is much more important among big market cap firms, 82% of large firms were revised upwards and 76% were revised downwards.

Abnormal Returns in the Post-Event Period

Table 7 reports the post-event long-term market performance for the upwardly (downwardly) revised companies in Panel A (Panel B) for a period *k*

= *1, 2, ..., 24* months. Benchmark excess returns are estimated as the difference of buy-and-hold returns for the CG score revised companies and the performance of the size over book-to-market reference portfolio.

Panel A of Table 7 shows that during the 24-month period following a third CG score revision, the ABHAR of the upwardly revised companies are statistically null. This result indicates an absence of long-term overperformance or underperformance for the upwardly revised companies in the post-event period. Therefore, hypothesis 1a of zero long-term abnormal returns for portfolios of companies with upward CG revisions is not rejected over the post-revision period. Figures 1a illustrates these results.

Table 7. ABHARs following the revised CG score size and book-to-market reference portfolio

Panel A : Post Upward Revision ABHAR & Size/BtM reference portfolios

Month	μ	σ	tsa	n
1	0.4%	0.079	0.485	132
2	0.5%	0.109	0.474	132
3	-0.1%	0.123	-0.083	132
4	1.0%	0.133	0.878	132
5	1.8%	0.158	1.338	132
6	2.8%	0.239	1.625	132
7	1.9%	0.185	1.197	132
8	2.4%	0.191	1.514	132
9	2.4%	0.204	1.399	132
10	3.0%	0.221	1.602	132
11	3.2%	0.227	1.606	127
12	2.8%	0.227	1.404	127
13	1.7%	0.244	0.812	126
14	1.8%	0.262	0.795	123
15	1.3%	0.274	0.550	123
16	0.3%	0.288	0.141	120
17	0.5%	0.309	0.173	117
18	1.5%	0.333	0.497	117
19	0.6%	0.338	0.203	117
20	-0.3%	0.355	-0.072	115
21	-0.5%	0.373	-0.119	103
22	0.1%	0.431	0.059	99
23	-0.3%	0.510	-0.010	99
24	-1.1%	0.562	-0.109	96

Panel B : Post Downward Revision ABHAR & Size/BtM reference portfolios

Month	μ	σ	tsa	n
1	0.5%	0.063	0.872***	120
2	0.0%	0.098	0.066***	120
3	-0.7%	0.104	-0.738***	120
4	-2.0%	0.111	-1.915***	120
5	-3.1%	0.127	-2.650***	120
6	-3.3%	0.144	-2.488***	120
7	-3.9%	0.160	-2.538***	120
8	-4.4%	0.163	-2.908***	120
9	-5.0%	0.179	-3.048***	120
10	-5.0%	0.198	-2.723***	120
11	-4.5%	0.213	-2.211***	118
12	-5.0%	0.220	-2.372***	118
13	-5.9%	0.236	-2.495***	118
14	-6.7%	0.224	-3.049***	117
15	-7.1%	0.231	-3.130***	116
16	-8.7%	0.234	-3.857***	115
17	-8.7%	0.234	-3.937***	112
18	-7.5%	0.265	-3.011***	112
19	-6.5%	0.290	-2.397***	112
20	-8.6%	0.289	-3.218***	111
21	-8.2%	0.293	-2.996***	106
22	-9.8%	0.309	-3.339***	104
23	-9.6%	0.323	-3.137***	104
24	-9.6%	0.339	-2.996***	103

This table presents the difference in returns for revised CG score companies against the benchmark—the size and book-to-market reference portfolio—in the post-event period. In Panel A (Panel B), the sample under examination comprises 132 (120) equities that were upwardly (downwardly) revised at least three times among the 600 selected European firms. The BHARs are calculated over the period 1997–2009 and are defined as the differences in the change in wealth for investors that hold shares in a revised CG score company compared to the benchmark for an investment holding period of $k = 1, 2, \ldots, 24$ months following the event. To solve the problem of positive skewness present in the buy-and-hold methodology and associated with the comparison of individual securities' returns to those of broad benchmarks, we adopt t-statistics calculated using the skewness-adjusted methodology introduced by Lyon, Barber, and Tsai (1999). The superscripts *, **, and *** indicate significance at the 10%, 5%, and 1% levels, respectively.

Stoxx 600 : Mean Buy-and-Hold Abnormal Returns after Upward Revisions on Corporate Governance scores

Size and Book-to-market reference portfolios

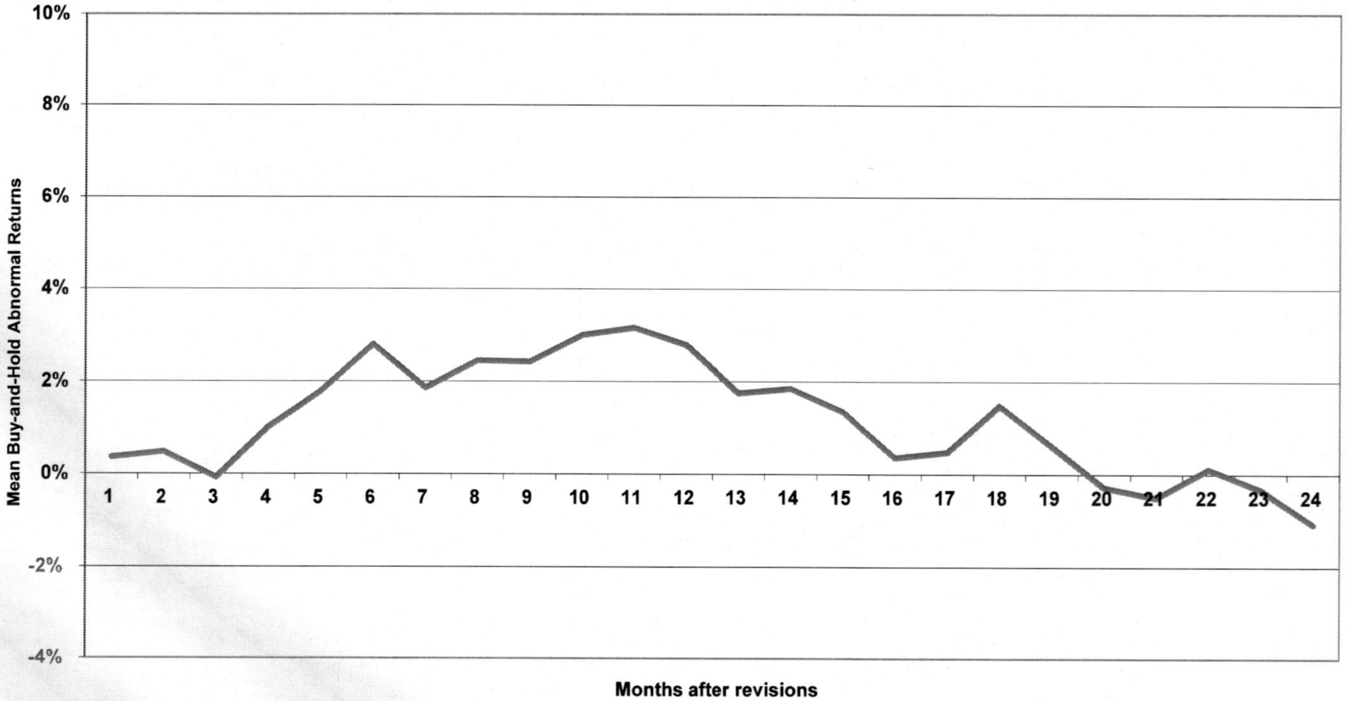

Sources : Natixis AM, Vigeo, data 12.1996 - 11.2009 - DJ Stoxx 600 panel

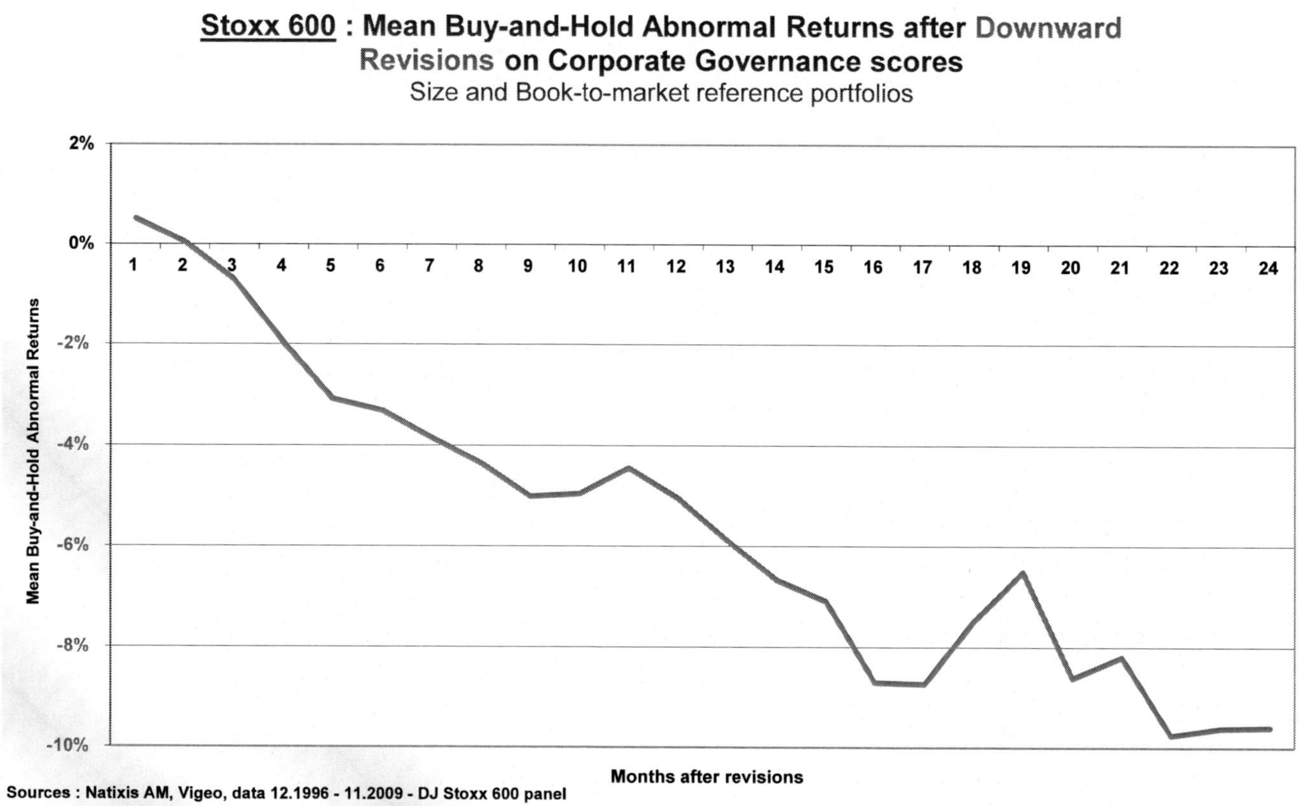

Figure 1. ABHARs following the revised CG score size and book-to-market reference portfolio.

Stoxx 600 : Tracking error after Upward Revisions on Corporate Governance scores

Size and Book-to-market reference portfolios

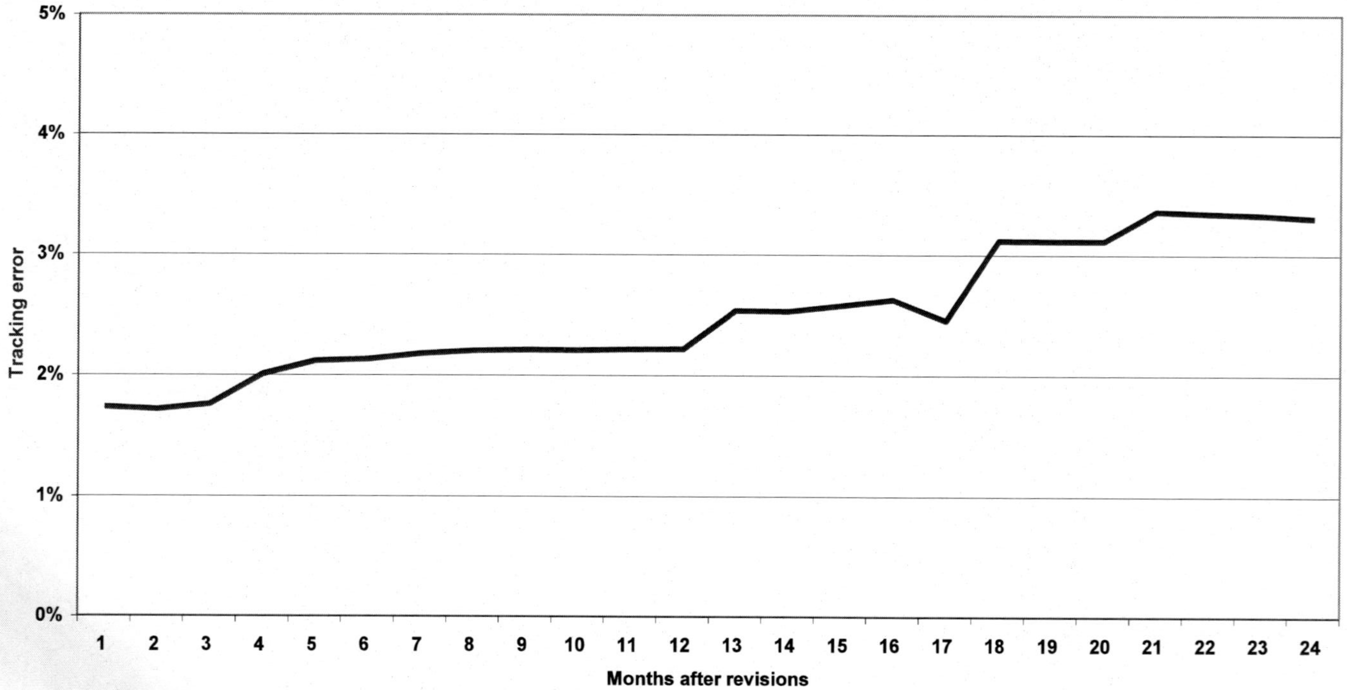

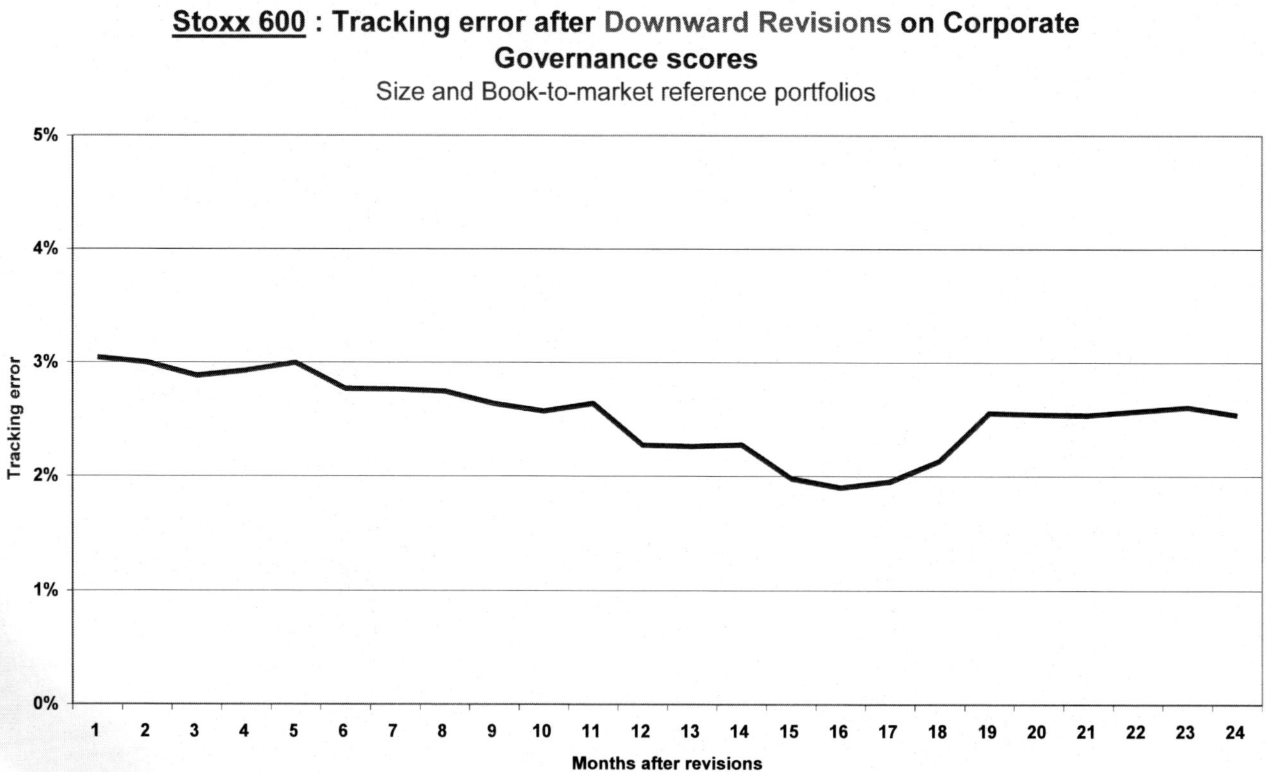

Figure 2. Tracking-error volatility following the revised CG score size and book-to-market reference portfolio.

Table 8. Tracking-error volatility following the revised CG scores

Month	1	2	3	4	5	6	7	8	9	10	11	12	13
Upward Revision TEV & Size/BtM reference portfolios	1.7%	1.7%	1.8%	2.0%	2.1%	2.1%	2.2%	2.2%	2.2%	2.2%	2.2%	2.2%	2.5%
Downward Revision TEV & Size/BtM reference portfolios	3.0%	3.0%	2.9%	2.9%	3.0%	2.8%	2.8%	2.7%	2.6%	2.6%	2.6%	2.3%	2.3%

Month	14	15	16	17	18	19	20	21	22	23	24
Upward Revision TEV & Size/BtM reference portfolios	2.5%	2.6%	2.6%	2.5%	3.1%	3.1%	3.1%	3.4%	3.3%	3.3%	3.3%
Downward Revision TEV & Size/BtM reference portfolios	2.3%	2.0%	1.9%	2.0%	2.1%	2.6%	2.5%	2.5%	2.6%	2.6%	2.5%

This table presents the tracking-error volatility (TEV) relative to reference portfolios for revised CG score companies over the post-event period. The tracking-error volatility measures how closely a portfolio of revised companies follows the reference portfolio against which it is benchmarked. The tracking-error volatility is calculated as the standard deviation of the difference in returns between the portfolio and the size and book-to-market reference portfolio. The sample under examination comprises 132 (120) companies that were upwardly (downwardly) revised at least three times among the 600 European firms selected.

In Figure 1a the sample comprises 132 equities with CG scores that were upwardly revised at least three times and in Figure 1b the sample comprises 120 equities with CG scores that were downwardly revised at least three times among the 600 European firms selected. The ABHAR is that of revised CG scores companies after the event month. The BHAR for security *i* over the holding period *k* is mathematically defined as

$$BHAR_{i,k} = \prod_{t=1}^{k}(1 + r_{i,t}) - \prod_{t=1}^{k}(1 + r_{rpi,t})$$

where $r_{i,t}$ is the total return in security *i* at month *t* and $r_{pi,t}$ is the return of the size and book-to-market reference portfolio.

In Figure 5a the sample comprises 132 equities with CG scores that were upwardly revised at least three times after the event month and in Figure 5b the sample comprises 120 equities with CG scores that were downwardly revised at least three times after the event month among the 600 European firms selected. The tracking-error volatility (TEV) is calculated as the monthly standard deviation of the difference in returns between the portfolio and the size and book-to-market reference portfolio on the last 24 monthly returns. The tracking-error volatility is mathematically defined as

$$TEV = \sigma(R_{p,t} - R_{b,t}) = \sqrt{\frac{\sum_{t=1}^{n}(R_{p,t} - R_{b,t})^2}{n}}$$

where $r_{p,t}$ is the monthly return of the revised CG score portfolio at month *t* and $r_{b,t}$ is the monthly return of the size and book-to-market reference portfolio, with *n* the number of months retained in the calculation of the standard deviation.

Panel B of Table 7 shows that the stock market performance of downwardly revised companies deteriorates significantly during the post-event period. The ABHAR ranges from -5.0% after a 12-month period, down to -8.7% and -9.6% after 16 and 24 months respectively, following the third revision event. In terms of statistical significance, the skewness-adjusted t-statistics for those two last abnormal returns—t_{sa} values of -3.857 and -2.996 respectively—are both significant at the 1% level. Therefore, hypothesis 1b of zero long-term abnormal returns for portfolios of companies with downward CG revisions is rejected over the post-revision period. It appears that the accumulation of bad news related to downwardly revised CG scores triggers a long-term negative reaction. Figures 1b illustrates these results.

Evidence of zero abnormal returns for the upwardly revised companies and robust negative abnormal returns for the downwardly revised companies suggest asymmetry in investor behavior. The next section analyzes the risk—the tracking-error—of these two sub-samples over the post-event period.

Tracking-Error Volatility

This section examines the risk associated with the returns by focusing on the tracking-error volatility. It is calculated as the monthly standard deviation of the difference in returns between the portfolio and the benchmark on the last 24 monthly returns. Table 8 first reports the tracking-error volatility relative to the size and book-to-market reference portfolios for upwardly revised CG companies over the post-event period.

Results show that during the 24-month period following the third revision, the tracking errors of the upwardly revised companies evolve in a range between 1.7% to 3.4%, with an upward trend. We notice an increase in tracking errors over the post-event period; however, the levels of the tracking errors of this investment strategy remain moderate. As illustrated in Figure 2a, the rolling tracking errors evolve in a rather small interval after the post-upward revision period of 24 months. These results underline a slight increase in risk taking during this period. However, this increase in tracking errors is not rewarded by positive abnormal returns (see Panel A of Table 7 and Figure 1a). Therefore, investing in upwardly revised companies does not seem to be an effective strategy.

Table 8 also shows that the tracking errors of the downwardly revised companies evolve in a range between 3% and 1.9%, with a slight downward trend. Overall, the levels of the tracking errors of this investment strategy remain moderate. As illustrated in Figure 2b, the rolling tracking errors evolve in a rather small interval after the post-downward revision period of 24 months. These results confirm the stability of the relative volatility to the benchmark, underlining relatively low risk taking. Moreover, this slight decrease in tracking errors is rewarded by negative abnormal returns (see Panel B of Table 7 and Figure 1b). Therefore, investing in downwardly revised companies by short-selling their stocks seems an effective strategy.

We argue that CG scores improvement (degradation) is associated with the implementation of better (worst) CG practices. Better practices often result in more transparency in the eyes of the shareholders. By being more transparent, firms take the risk of revealing information to financial markets that could potentially harm their business. This could explain that the tracking error of the positively revised firms rises slightly during the 24 months after the event-month. Conversely, lower CG scores often echo less transparency towards investors, which in turn results in less idiosyncratic risk for these firms. This could explain why the tracking error of the negatively revised firms slightly diminishes during the 24 months after the event-month.

Table 9 shows the impact of downward revisions on subsequent returns for the top (Q1 – Panel A) and lowest (Q4 – Panel B) CG scores quartiles. The distribution of subsequent returns for with the highest CG score (Q1) is much greater, most notably after 12 months. This asymmetric behavior of subsequent returns between high and low levels of CG scores firms should nevertheless be considered cautiously since the sample of Q1 firms includes a very small number of observations.

Table 9. ABHARs of equities revised downward at least three times and Quartiles of CG Scores

Panel A : Post Downward Revision ABHAR among Q1 - Top Quartile of CG scores

Month	μ	σ	tsa	n
1	5,1%	0,091	1.304	4
4	3,8%	0,125	0.575	4
8	-9,6%	0,125	-1.657*	4
12	-9,8%	0,088	-2.857***	4
16	-21,6%	0,083	-5.204***	3
20	-20,4%	0,055	-9.400***	3
24	-30,0%	0,026	-6.793***	3

Panel B : Post Downward Revision ABHAR among Q4 - Bottom Quartile of CG scores

Month	μ	σ	tsa	n
1	0,9%	0,063	1.001	49
4	-2,3%	0,106	-1.476	49
8	-5,5%	0,152	-2.419**	49
12	-7,2%	0,186	-2.612***	48
16	-11,3%	0,232	-3.741***	48
20	-9,7%	0,334	-2.067**	48
24	-10,7%	0,394	-1.917*	44

CONCLUSION

In recent years, CG has received increased attention in great part due to highly publicized corporate scandals and their disastrous consequences for stakeholders. However, with a few notable exceptions discussed above, the finance literature lacks empirical research on long-term performance studies focusing on the relation between *changes* in CG scores and financial performance. Moreover, understanding and anticipating investor behavior can help design profitable investment strategies. Our findings suggest that the market reaction to repeated CG revisions depends on their direction, be they upward or downward.

The impact of upward revisions on equities appears not to be followed by sustainable significant positive abnormal returns. Furthermore, the absence of abnormal returns is not accompanied by a reduction in tracking-error volatility but, instead, a slight increase. Therefore, designing a stock portfolio based on upwardly revised companies is unlikely to be a profitable investment strategy.

But, the impact of downward CG revisions on stock prices appears to be followed by sustainable significant negative abnormal returns. This could be explained by the fact that investors are generally loss averse (Tversky and Kahneman, 1992); they care more about potential losses than potential gains. This leads them to hold on to portfolios with declining values in the hope of recovering their losses. These robust abnormal returns are accompanied by a weak and almost unchanged level of tracking-error volatility over the post-event period. Therefore, short-selling stocks of companies that experience downward CG score revisions could be a profitable investment strategy.

These results contribute to our understanding of the relation between CG changes and financial performance and provide a basis for future work in several ways. The CG data used in this study are aggregate scores of four sub-criteria of CG: the board of directors, audit and internal controls, shareholders, and executive remuneration. Each of these four criteria is also an aggregate scores on relevant governance provisions.[1] The lack of Vigeo monthly data over the period of our study does not allow carrying out a statistical study to draw rigorous conclusions on the impact of sub-criterion scores changes on subsequent returns. Futures studies with larger time series of sub-criteria of CG scores should aim at identifying the specific CG factors that affect financial markets in terms of risk and returns. Future work should also further

[1] See the Appendix.

investigate the presence of asymmetry between firms according to their CG score level.

APPENDIX 1. VIGEO CORPORATE GOVERNANCE CRITERIA

1 Board of Directors

Definition

Enterprise commits to set up a board of directors with the capability of controlling and advising executives and to be held accountable to shareholders.

Principles for Action

A. Ensure that the board is able to exercise appropriate control over top management.

B. Ensure that the board is held accountable to company shareholders.

2. Audit and Internal Controls

Definition

Assesses enterprise commitment to establish efficient systems for risk tracking and risk assessment and to produce strategic internal information. Assesses the extent to which this commitment is reflected in financial information provided to the public. The board of directors is responsible for the objectivity and relevance of the system.

Principles for Action

A. Ensure that financial information provided to the public is accurate and that company risks are appropriately managed.

B. Ensure that an audit committee/function is in place to manage the above-mentioned issues.

3. Shareholder Rights

Definition

Assesses enterprise commitment to ensure the fair treatment of shareholders, who should be able to actively exercise appropriate control over strategic decision making. Rules pertaining to shareholding and shareholder rights to participate in general meetings are of fundamental importance.

Principles for Action

A. Ensure the fair and equal treatment of all shareholders and respect the principle of one share, one vote.

B. Guarantee the rights of shareholders to participate in the annual general meeting and to adopt resolutions.

C. Promote and facilitate the exercise of voting rights.

4. Executive Remuneration

Definition

Assesses enterprise commitment to use executive remuneration as a tool to improve congruence between executives' and shareholders' interests.

Principles for Action

Ensure that executive remuneration is used as a tool to align the interests of executives with those of company shareholders.

REFERENCES

Aggarwal, R., Erel, E., Stulz, R., and Williamson, R. (2008), 'Differences in Governance Practices between US and Foreign Firms: Measurement, Causes, and Consequences,' *Review of Financial Studies*, Vol. 22, No. 8, pp. 3131–3169.

Barber, B. M., and Lyon, J. D. (1997), 'Detecting Long-Run Abnormal Stock Returns: The Empirical Power and Specification of Test Statistics,' *Journal of Financial Economics*, Vol. 43, No. 3, pp. 341–372.

Bassen, A., Prigge, S., and Zöllner, C. (2008), 'Behind Broad Corporate Governance Aggregates: A First Look at Single Provisions of the German

Corporate Governance Code,' April, SSRN 965355, available at http://ssrn.com/abstract=965355.

Bauer, R., Günster, N., and Otten, R. (2004), 'Empirical Evidence on Corporate Governance in Europe: The Effect on Stock Returns, Firm Value and Performance,' *Journal of Asset Management*, Vol. 5, No. 2, pp. 91–104.

Bebchuk, L. A., Cohen, A., and Ferrell, A. (2009), 'What Matters in Corporate Governance?,' *Review of Financial Studies*, Vol. 22, No. 2, pp. 783–827.

Bebchuck, L., Cohen A., and Wang, C (2012), 'Learning and the Disappearing Association between Governance and Returns,' *Journal of Financial Economics*, Vol. 108, pp. 323–348.

Beiner, S., Drobetz, W., Schmid, M. M., and Zimmermann, H. (2006), 'An Integrated Framework of Corporate Governance and Firm Valuation,' *European Financial Management*, Vol. 12, pp. 249–283.

Bhagat, S., and Bolton, B. J. (2008), 'Corporate Governance and Firm Performance,' *Journal of Corporate Finance*, Vol. 14, No. 3, pp. 257–273.

Brown, L. D., and Caylor, M. L. (2006), 'Corporate Governance and Firm Valuation,' *Journal of Accounting and Public Policy*, Vol. 25, No. 4, pp. 409–434.

Brown, L. D., and Caylor, M. L. (2009), 'Corporate Governance and Firm Operating Performance,' *Review of Quantitative Finance and Accounting*, Vol. 32, No. 2, pp. 129–144.

Carhart, M. M. (1997), 'On Persistence in Mutual Fund Performance,' *Journal of Finance*, Vol. 52, No. 1, pp. 57–82.

Cellier, A., and Chollet, P. (2011): 'The Impact of Corporate Social Responsibility Rating Announcements on European Stock Prices,' AFFI International Conference, Montpellier, 11th to 13th May. http://papers.ssrn.com/sol3/papers.cfm?abstract_id=1836902.

Cellier, A., and Chollet, P. (2012), 'CSR Rating Information: Relevance and Impacts on Financial,' in "Board Directors and Corporate Social Responsibility", MacMillan Palgrave.

Chang, Y., and Chan, C. (2008), 'Financial analysts' stock recommendation revisions and stock price changes,' *Applied Financial Economics*, Vol. 18, pp. 309-325.

Charreaux, G., and Desbrières, P. (1998), 'Gouvernance des entreprises: valeur partenariale contre valeur actionnariale,' *Finance Contrôle Stratégie*, Vol. 1, No. 2, pp. 57–88.

Cheung Y.-L., Connelly, J. T., Jiang, P., and Limpaphayom, P. (2011), 'Does Corporate Governance Predict Future Performance? Evidence from Hong Kong,' *Financial Management*, Vol. 40, pp. 159–197.

Cheung Y.-L., Jiang, P., Limpaphayom, P., and Lu, T. (2010), 'Corporate Governance in China: A Step Forward,' *European Financial Management*, Vol. 16, No 1, pp. 94–123.

Chhaochharia, V., and Laeven, L. A. (2009), 'Corporate Governance, Norms and Practices,' *Journal of Financial Intermediation*, Vol. 18, No. 3, pp. 405–431.

Chincarini, L. B., and Daehwan, K. (2006), *Quantitative Equity Portfolio Management: An Active Approach to Portfolio Construction and Management*. McGraw-Hill.

Clacher, I., Doriye, E., and Hillier, D. (2008), 'Does Corporate Governance Matter? New Evidence from the United Kingdom,' November, SSRN 1293188, available at http://ssrn.com/abstract=1293188.

Core, J., Guay, W., and Rusticus, T. (2006), 'Does Weak Governance Cause Weak Stock Returns? An Examination of Firm Operating Performance and Investors' Expectations,' *Journal of Finance*, Vol. 61, No. 2, pp. 655–687.

Doidge, C., Karolyi, G. A., and Stulz, R. M. (2007), 'Why Do Countries Matter so Much for Corporate Governance?,' *Journal of Financial Economics*, Vol. 86, No. 1, pp. 1–39.

Drobetz, W., Schillhofer, A., and Zimmermann, H. (2004), 'Corporate Governance and Expected Stock Returns: Evidence from Germany,' *European Financial Management*, Vol. 10, pp. 267–293.

Fama, E. F. (1998), 'Market Efficiency, Long-Term Returns, and Behavioral Finance,' *Journal of Financial Economics*, Vol. 49, No. 1, pp. 283–306.

Fama, E. F., and French, K. R. (1992), 'The Cross-Section of Expected Stock Returns,' *Journal of Finance*, Vol. 47, No. 2, pp. 427–465.

Fama, E. F., and K. R. French (1993), 'Common Risk Factors in the Returns on Bonds and Stocks,' *Journal of Financial Economics*, Vol. 33, pp. 3–56.

Girerd-Potin, I. Jimenez-Garcès, S. and Louvet, P. (2014), 'Which Dimensions of Social Responsibility Concern Financial Investors?,' *Journal of Business Ethics*, Vol. 121, pp. 559-576.

Gleason, C. A., and Lee, C. M. (2003), 'Analyst Forecast Revisions and Market Price Discovery. *The Accounting Review*, Vol. 78, No. 1, pp. 193–225.

Gompers, P. A., Ishii, J., and Metrick, A. (2003), 'Corporate Governance and Equity Prices,' *Quarterly Journal of Economics*, Vol. 118, No. 1, pp. 107–155.

Gompers, P. A., and Lerner, J. (2003), 'The Really Long-Run Performance of Initial Public Offerings: The Pre-Nasdaq Evidence,' *Journal of Finance*, Vol. 58, No. 4, pp. 1355–1392.

Green, T.C. (2006), 'The value of client access to analyst recommendations,' *Journal of Financial and Quantitative Analysis*, Vol. 41, No. 1, pp. 1-24.

Grinold, R. C., and Kahn, R. N. (1989), *Active Portfolio Management: A Quantitative Approach for Providing Returns and Controlling Risk*, 2nd ed. McGraw-Hill.

Johnson, N. J. (1978), 'Modified t Tests and Confidence Intervals for Asymmetrical Populations,' *Journal of the American Statistical Association*, Vol. 73, pp. 536–544.

Johnson, S. A., Moorman, T., and Sorescu, S. (2009), 'A Re-examination of Corporate Governance and Equity Prices,' *Review of Financial Studies*, Vol. 22, pp. 4753–4786.

Klapper, L. F., and Love, I. (2004), 'Corporate Governance, Investor Protection, and Performance in Emerging Markets,' *Journal of Corporate Finance*, Vol. 10, pp. 703–728.

Kothari, S. P., and Warner, J. B. (1997), 'Measuring Long-Horizon Security Price Performance,' *Journal of Financial Economics*, Vol. 43, No. 3, pp. 301–339.

Lyon, J. D., Barber, B. M., and Tsai, C.-L. (1999), 'Improved Methods for Tests of Long-Run Abnormal Stock Returns,' *Journal of Finance*, Vol. 54, No. 1, pp. 165–201.

Mitchell, M. L., and Stafford, E. (2000), 'Managerial Decisions and Long-Term Stock Price Performance,' *Journal of Business*, Vol. 73, No. 3, pp. 287–320.

Organisation for Economic Co-operation and Development (2004), *Principles of Corporate Governance*, Organization of Economic Cooperation and Development.

Philippon, T. (2006), 'Corporate Governance over the Business Cycle,' *Journal of Economic Dynamics and Control*, Vol. 30, No. 11, pp. 2117–2141.

Pope, P., and Yadav, P. (1994), 'Discovering Errors in Tracking Error,' *Journal of Portfolio Management*, Vol. 20, No. 2, pp. 27–32.

Roll, R. (1992), 'A Mean/Variance Analysis of Tracking Error,' *Journal of Portfolio Management*, Vol. 18, No. 4, pp. 13–22.

Sloan, R., 'Do stock prices fully reflect information in accruals and cash flows about future earnings? *The Accounting Review*, Vol. 71, 1996, pp. 289–315.

Tversky, A., and Kahneman, D. (1992), 'Advances in Prospect Theory: Cumulative Representation of Uncertainty,' *Journal of Risk and Uncertainty*, Vol. 5, No. 4, pp. 297–323.

Xie, H., 'The mispricing of abnormal accruals,' *The Accounting Review*, Vol. 76, 2001, pp. 357–74.

In: Financial Performance
Editor: Elaine Moreno
ISBN: 978-1-63484-501-4

Chapter 4

DOES FINANCIAL ACCESSIBILITY AND INCLUSION PROMOTE ECONOMIC GROWTH IN LOW INCOME COUNTRIES (LICS)?

***Francis K. Agyekum**, Stuart Locke*[1] *and Nirosha Hewa Wellalage*[2]**
University of Waikato Management School, Hamilton, New Zealand

ABSTRACT

This study examines the link between financial inclusion, development and economic growth in low income countries (LICs). The analysis is quantitative, covering the period 1998-2013 and uses International Financial Statistics (IFS) and Bankscope data from the World Bank database. The use of a quantile regressions model in the analysis provides an extra level of robustness from earlier work and illuminates some interesting issues regarding the impact of financial inclusion. Depth of financial inclusion is significant in relation to economic growth compared with financial market depth. The study provides a strong case that the potential growth effect of financial institutions (banks) in LICs is much stronger relative to that of the financial market. Within the LIC context, the growth-enhancing effect of the financial sector thrives on the synergy of the financial institutions as it

* Francis K. Agyekum, PhD Candidate. E-mail: fka3@students.waikato.ac.nz.
[1] Stuart Locke, Professor of Finance. E-mail: smlocke@waikato.ac.nz.
[2] Nirosha Hewa Wellalage, Senior Lecturer, Finance. E-mail: nirosha@waikato.ac.nz.

engenders wider inclusion. A significant outcome of this work is an increased appreciation of the importance of thorough analysis and the many cross dependencies. For policy makers there is a clear signal; don't develop plans around stimulating or reducing just one instrument in the economy and expect non-confounding results. The light shed on these key relationships suggest that policies on growth, financial sector reforms and financial inclusion need not be implemented in isolation. This is especially the case in LICs where institutional bottlenecks and structural constraints often widen the existing exclusion gap.

Keywords: financial inclusion, financial structure, financial development, LICs, economic growth, quantile regression

INTRODUCTION

This chapter investigates how financial inclusion and deepening contributes to the economic growth in a specific lower income country (LIC). The question of whether financial accessibility and inclusion promotes economic growth has not been adequately addressed in prior research. This general lack of appropriate empirical response to the above question is even more pronounced in developing LICs. The study is therefore motivated by the lack of sound empirical work exploring this linkage for LICs. Ghana provides a useful case study.

Financial inclusion captures the availability and accessibility of credit at reasonable cost to the poor and the marginalised in society, including small businesses. Financial inclusion, and in particular access to credit, intuitively suggests that it should stimulate economic activity. However, the concept of financial inclusion is broader than just credit accessibility. In particular, access to credit as a natural outcome of a deepened financial system is of interest, especially within the context of how this form of inclusion can foster economic growth and development in LICs.

The puzzle is, what drives growth? Is it the capital market, especially the stock exchange that provides liquidity to the market and signals a pricing of risk? Alternatively, is the financial institutions, and in particular the extent of financial inclusion, the source of growth? For LICs it is important to maximise successes, so where to concentrate effort is important. This paper addresses the issue and offers an answer. Causality testing is provided to the best extent possible given the datasets available. In the future more data may provide opportunities for further robustness testing of this model, including for example the use of generalised method of moment (GMM).

The exact mechanism through which financial inclusion and deepening impact growth is a complex subject that has mixed outcomes. Research that holds financial development does not influence the growth process asserts that finance naturally follows where enterprise leads (Robinson, 1952). Finance will, therefore, only respond to real sector demands and cannot be a key determinant of growth (Levine, 2005). Alternatively, there is a view that ignoring the contribution of the financial sector towards growth is not justifiable. Following what became known as the 'McKinnon-Shaw (1973) hypothesis' of financial liberalisation, Gockel and Akoena (2002) suggest that Ghana's financial sector reform undertaken in 1988, as did most developing nations (Adu, Marbuah, & Mensah, 2013), recognises the role finance plays in growth process of a country. The current study considers how finance matters in the economic development process, especially in developing economies where structural constraints prevail.

Economic growth is stimulated when the financial system addresses information asymmetry and transaction costs as means to improve relationships with participants in the real sector of the economy. The crucial role that the financial system plays towards growth is seen in the light of financial arrangements, ranging from contract enforcement, market mechanism and intermediation processes, all geared towards addressing the structural rigidities and market imperfections inherent in most countries, especially LICs. The point has been emphasised that these arrangements facilitate mobilisation of domestic savings, guarantee liquidity and ensure efficient managements of risk all as means to getting potential investment opportunities nurtured (Demirgüç-Kunt & Levine, 2008; Pietrovito, 2009).

As potential investment opportunities are identified and included financially through credit extension, the financial system plays a role when it aligns, and in some cases alters, incentives that firms face resulting in economic growth. There is ample empirical evidence to back the view that firms in advanced financial systems face fewer constraints when raising external financing for expansion and growth than firms in underdeveloped ones (Beck & Demirguc-Kunt, 2006; Beck, Demirgüç-Kunt, & Maksimovic, 2005; Demirgüç-Kunt, 2006; Love, 2003).

Focusing on financial deepening, which engenders inclusion as a conduit for promoting economic growth, does not diminish the important roles that the legal and regulatory framework, resource endowments and the political environment play towards the same end. Empirically highlighting the role financial inclusion as a result of a deepened financial system plays in the growth prospects of LICs underscores policy ramifications supported by this study. The conclusion that financial inclusion has the potential to drive economic growth as financial resources become widely accessible to the greater number of the population is important. Policies strengthening the drive towards attaining broader inclusion in developing economies are essential. Financial inclusion could be one of the top 10 priorities of policy-makers aiming to promote growth in LICs. As detailed attention is paid to understanding the finance-growth nexus from the perspective of an LIC, this study separates itself from other works because they use cross-country data, often missing out detailed, unique and individual country developmental characteristics.

The method of analysis used in this study also contributes in a significant way to our understanding of the underlying relationships. The method produces robust outcomes (Cameron & Trivedi, 2005; Wellalage & Locke, 2014), as quantile regression with similar attributes to ordinary least square (OLS) allows one to investigate the entire distribution of the real per capita GDP indicator (dependent variable) rather than its conditional mean as OLS does (Cameron & Trivedi, 2005). Juxtaposing this outcome with a generalised least square model (GLM) adds more insights to its robustness, given that some key classical linear regression assumptions which strictly guide OLS might be in violation, hence the use of GLM.

A review of James Ang's work that surveys a recent literature relating to finance-growth relationship (Ang, 2008) revealed a methodological gap this present study fills. Of about forty-nine (49) literature spanning from 1969 to 2008 surveyed, only one used semiparametric partial linear model which was not necessarily quantile regression. The use of QR in this study therefore becomes a methodological innovation that has since been missing from finance-growth literature.

FINANCIAL SECTOR LIBERALISATION: EVIDENCE FROM GHANA

In the late 1980s, Ghana undertook financial sector reform as part of the broader Structural Adjustment Program (SAP) supported by the Britton Woods Institutions. At that time the existing banks were in a distressed condition. There was a pressing need for action and steps were taken to reform the sector. Issues relating to the direct control of interest rates[1], directed allocation of financial resources to priority sectors and the dominance of public sector banks[2] were addressed. The reforms brought a liberalisation of credit controls on banks, deregulating the interest rate ceiling, reforms to regulations and prudential supervision and a restructuring of insolvent banks.

The controls in many respects created unintended outcomes. The credit control policy that compelled banks to lend to administratively determined priority sectors such as agriculture resulted in a slowing of financial inclusion. Non-priority sectors were financially excluded, especially foreign firms that needed to obtain Central Bank permits before accessing credit from domestic financial intermediaries (Brownbridge & Gockel, 1996), provides a further illustration of potentially unintended results.

Figure 1 below shows the effect of the pre-reform rigid polices, and the impact that the financial sector reform brought on both the financial and the real sector indicators. In essence, it reveals the various phases of the financial developments in Ghana both pre- and post-reform eras. The reforms impacted both the financial sector and the nonfinancial sector. In Figure 1, the response of several financial indicators is traced through the pre-reform to the post-reform period.

Included in the series are bank credit to private sector as ratio of GDP, bank credits to deposit ratio, banks assets as percentage of GDP, monetary growth rate, inflation rate and bank deposits as percentage of GDP. Whereas inflation was in an upward spiral over the period prior to the reforms, key monetary and financial indicators depicted downward trends. The positive impact of the reform is noticeable. The period following reform produced not only declining rates of inflation but, most significantly, the upward movements in almost all the key financial indicators.

The establishment and opening of the Ghana Stock Exchange in the early 1990s provided a further injection of new dynamism into the post-reform financial sector.

---

[1] Prior to the reform in the late 1980s, the Central bank determined both minimum deposits rates and maximum lending rates. In some cases, real interest rates tend to be negative as the nominal interest rate were administratively fixed below the prevailing inflation.

[2] Brownbridge, M. and Gockel, A. F. (1996) commenting on the dominance nature of the public sector in the financial system, indicate that between 1950 and 1980, all of the banks established were either complete state-ownership or majority ownership by the public sector, coupled with the fact that the state had to own minority shares in the two foreign banks that were already established in the mid-1970s.

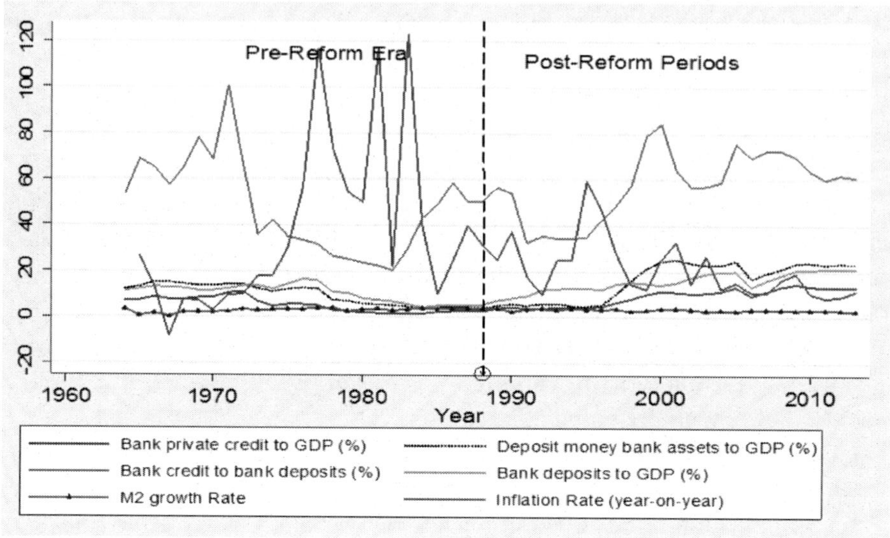

Figure 1. How financial indicators responded to the Financial Sector Adjustments Program.

FINANCIAL DEVELOPMENT, INCLUSION AND ECONOMIC GROWTH NEXUS: THEORETICAL FOUNDATION

Scholarly research interest in the finance-growth nexus is often traced to pioneering work of Joseph Schumpeter in the 1911/12. Schumpeter exploresd the role of credit towards entrepreneurship and how that could spur up growth (Schumpeter, 1934). Schumpeter's ground-breaking work on the subject formed the strong foundation for others like Gurley and Shaw (1955), Goldsmith (1969), and later McKinnon (1973) to build on. Recent empirical studies have approached the debate between finance and growth from an endogenous growth model (Bencivenga & Smith, 1991; Chakraborty & Ray, 2006; Levine, 2005). The model posits that real output growth depends on total factor productivity, capital stock, savings as well as the efficient functioning of the financial intermediaries that convert the mobilised savings into investments for deficit-spending units.

The link between financial inclusion and economic growth on the surface looks straightforward. However, there are multiple factors that come into play in terms of the financial system's efficiency in respect of generating appropriate signals to inform an optimal allocation of capital. Further, the role of monitoring a firm's performance and its corporate governance, mobilising and aggregating financial resources (savings) and finally effective risk pooling and amelioration, cannot be taken for granted (Levine, 2005). Is it the banks that dominate the growth process (bank-based view) or the financial market (market-based view) that drives the growth? Cohesion within the financial sector may be even more important and how each component plays a unique role contributes to the impact on economic growth (Levine, 2005). Theoretical basis for this more integrated financial function view is that financial markets or financial institutions, or both, are created in response to information and transaction costs as well as contract enforcement constraints.

The perspective of financial institutions and markets complementing each other in driving growth fits well with the early stages of economic development. Banks play an essential role in allocating financial resources in the early stages. As the economy develops and the financial sector evolves with more complex sets of financial arrangements for the now sophisticated clients, the role of financial markets emerges. Characteristically, banks are more inclined to funding less risky, more mature enterprises, whereas a financial market has the capacity to nurture new and more risky firms. The market is relatively endowed with a better set of risk management skills and expertise that allows the efficient adoption of risk ameliorating mechanisms. A deepened financial sector that engenders more inclusion may significantly contribute to economic growth.

The relationship between financial inclusion and economic development, according to Hannig and Jansen (2010), may be imperfect. Financial inclusion in simplest terms refers to the availability and accessibility of credit at reasonable cost to the poor and marginalised in society, including small businesses. As access to credit expands, a multiplier impact upon the economy becomes likely. The appreciation that the concept of inclusion is wider than just accessibility is essential. The financial process is inclusive, according to Sarma and Pais (2008), when it ensures availability, ease of access and usage of existing financial infrastructure by a broad range of people within society, regardless of their socio-economic status. Such a system promotes an efficient allocation of financial resources to productive use at an acceptable cost. This in turn advances economic growth and the development process. Viewed from the supply side, it may include provision of appropriate, affordable and widely accessible quality financial services to marginalised groups in society (Triki & Faye, 2013).

From the demand perspective however, financial inclusion may be thought of as the ability for every economic agent to access financial services that include an opportunity to save, make payments, transfer and access insurance services (Hannig & Jansen, 2010). Demirgüç-Kunt, Klapper, and van Oudheusden (2015) simply define it as the ability of individuals and firms to access and use formal financial services; and to Sarma and Pais (2011) it is a process which ensures that all active economic agents have access to and usage of a widely available formal financial system with fewer obstacles and less cost. Financial inclusion is therefore the ability of the previously 'unbanked' economic units (which includes both poor households and financially marginalised small firms) to access and fully participate in the formal financial system via the use of appropriate financial and technological platforms and services.

METHOD, RESULTS AND DISCUSSION

Data

Secondary data sources have been collected mainly from World Bank domain sources. Table 1 A, in the appendix section, gives detailed definition with sources, while Table 1 below depicts descriptive statistics of the data. The two main sources of data are World Bank Development Indicators-WDI and International Monetary Fund's (IMF) International Financial Statistics (IFS). The data covering the periods 1998-2013 are used for the empirical analysis. Though majority of the variables covered significantly longer periods as depicted by the summary descriptive statistics (see Table 1), others had a limited span, hence the sixteen (16) year data restriction. The descriptive statistics (see Table 1) and the Figure 1 reflect the fact that some data series span 1964-2013.

The size of the standard deviation of variables, such as inflation rate and the market capitalization (MCAP), points to distributional concerns over a few of the variables. Though the Kernel distribution plot (see Figure 2) indicates near symmetrical distribution for most of indicators, the skewness in some others partly motivated the use of GLM and quantile regression (QR) models instead of OLS.

Spearman's rank correlation matrix also highlights the key relations studied, especially with respect to the inclusion indicator and the economic growth variable. These non-parametric outcome of the studied variables, also reflects the strong and positive significant correlation[3] between the financial inclusion indicator (BC2PS) and economic growth indicator. The high correlation coefficient among some variables is an indication of the presence of a multicollinearity (with average VIF of approx. 8.8) problem, making the use of GLM and QR models fit better.

Method

The method of analysis is quantitative and the techniques used are micro-econometric. Regression methods are used including quantile regression (QR) and a generalized least-squared model (GLM). Both models are selected for their robustness given the datasets used. Koenker and Bassett (1978) developed QR as a robustness improvement upon ordinary least squares regression (OLS). QR is favoured in situations where observing the impact of incremental change in the independent variables (IVs) on the dependent variable (DV) at a specific quantile rather than at its conditional mean, as in OLS, is helpful.

Table 1. Descriptive and Summary Statistics

Variable	Obs[4]	Mean	Std. Dev.	Min	Max
Natural Log of GDP per capita	50	6.106318	.1879846	5.770731	6.633058
MCAP (% GDP)	23	13.5123	8.443061	1.150969	34.33479
BC2PS	50	8.041136	4.513014	1.542268	15.82746
LI	18	.3162912	.1218621	.015755	.479059
GSE T.O.R	21	3.509116	1.720347	1.221576	8.701888
Bank O. Cost	16	7.48625	1.430062	3.8	9.64
Inflation Rate	49	28.95075	28.1844	- 8.422486	122.8745
M2grwth	50	3.299363	.816089	.2100548	4.22727
REMI2GDP	35	.3247853	.2803306	.010476	.927455
NPA	16	14.53281	4.473782	6.4	22.7
Log FDI	24	19.37919	1.709765	16.51014	21.91553
U-rate	23	7.465217	2.883276	3.8	11
Sav2GDP	39	2.48321	.5055487	1.448533	3.365992

[3] Correlation coefficient of 0.8553* and is statistically significant at 5 percent level.
[4] The number of observations as given are the number of years the series reflect.

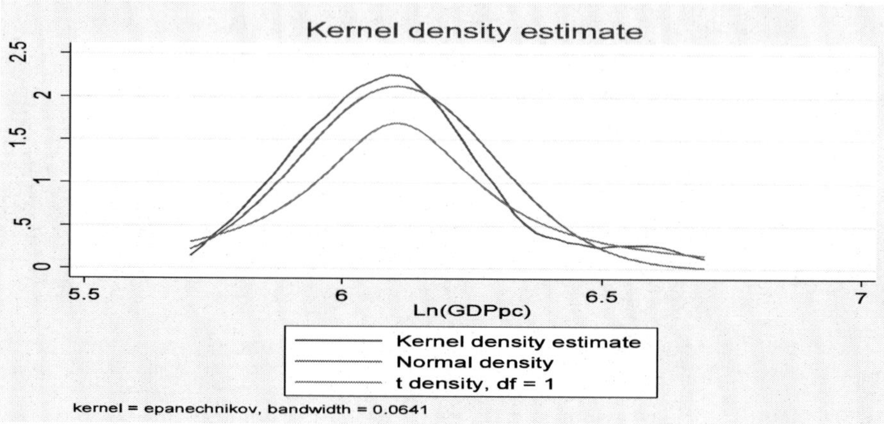

Figure 2. Kernel Density Estimates for the Dependent Variable.

The QR approach is an extremum estimator like the OLS (Cameron & Trivedi, 2005). However, unlike the latter, QR measures the relationship between y_i and x_i at a specific point on the conditional distribution of y_i (DV) in a way that gives a complete picture regarding the distribution of the dependent.

QR serves as a further robustness check for the GLM results. The quantile assumes a conditional distribution of a linear function of the regressors (Cameron & Trivedi, 2005) and avoids making assumptions about the parametric distribution of the errors. The model's insensitivity to outliers (Wellalage & Locke, 2014) as well as its suitability in situations where heteroscedasticity is inherent with the data (Cameron & Trivedi, 2005), adds to its strength. The flexibility it offers in allowing one to study the marginal impact of IVs on both location and scale parameters of the model, derives much deeper understanding of the data compared to the OLS and the GLM.

Model Specification

$$G = f\,(Fin\ Depth,\ Fin\ Effic,\ Fin/Mon\ Environ,\ SGD) \quad (1)$$

Where; G denotes economic growth, Fin Depth-Financial Depth, Fin Effic-Financial Efficiency, Fin/Mon Environ-Financial/monetary environment, controlling for SGD-standard growth determinants.

Dependent Variable

Dependent: G denotes *Economic Growth*, which is the dependent variable. Private sector credit to GDP ratio is favoured as a superior proxy of financial development and in our case inclusion. Adu et al. (2013) underscore in their study the sensitivity of growth-finance relationship to the proxy indicator for financial development/inclusion one adopts. Though broad money (M2 +) to GDP ratio has been used as proxy for financial development, there is increasing concern over it growth-inducing capacity. In keeping with this shift in thinking, and following prior studies (Beck & Levine, 2001, 2004; Ndako, 2010) we use natural log of real GDP per capita as proxy for economic growth indicator.

Independent Variables

1. *Financial Depth* captures both the "*financial inclusion*" (institution depths) and financial market depth. Measure of 'Financial Institutions Depth' captures the 'Financial Inclusion'; using private credit by deposit money banks to GDP (%;) whiles 'Financial Markets' Depth' is measured by 'Stock Market Capitalization.'
2. *Financial Efficiency* captured both market and institutional efficiencies. We proxied financial market efficiency by Stock Market (GSE[5]) Turnover Ratio (%); and financial institution's efficiency by Bank overhead costs to total assets (%).
3. *Financial/Monetary Environment* captures certain macroeconomic factors of either financial or monetary nature, which influences the growth process of the economy, defined below:
   a) *Monigrowth* - money and quasi money annual (%) growth;
   b) *Lerner Index (LI)* for banks, a proxy for competition in the banking financial sector.
   c) The rest of the variables include: Inflation rate, unemployment rate and private remittance inflows (% of GDP) and natural log of foreign direct investment flow and Banks Non-performing Assets (NPAs) and gross savings as percentage of GDP.

Specific Models Estimated

$$ln(GDPpc)_{\_t} = \beta_0 + \beta_1 MCAP_{\_t} + \beta_2 BC2PS_{\_t} + \beta_3 Remit_{\_t} + \beta_4 Infl_{\_t} + \beta_5 M2\ Growth_{\_t}, + \beta_6 LI_{\_t} + \beta_7 GSE_{T.O.R\_t} + \beta_8 U\_rate_{\_t} + \beta_9 lnFDI_{\_t} + \beta_{10} BOcost_t + \beta_{11} NPA_t + \beta_{12} \text{Sav2GDP}_t + e_t \quad (2)$$

Robustness Test: Using GLM as a benchmark, the study applied multiple models to investigate the variables of interest. Both the GLS model and the

[5] Ghana Stock Exchange.

quintile (least–absolute-value-LAV) model were used to estimate the growth equation to ensure more robustness. The Breusch-Pagan/Cook-Weisberg test for heteroscedasticity did reject the null-hypothesis that the error term is homoscedastic, warranting the use of QR and GLM.

The Durbin-Watson test for serial correlation is inconclusive. This necessitates running the residual graph to see the movement of the error term for the fitted model. This, coupled with the mean VIF 8.85, and presence of potential multicollinearity called for the use of GLM instead of OLS, benchmarking the results with the quantile regression model outcome.

Financial Structure and Development on Growth

Following Levine (2002) we specify growth equation;

Growth = f (Financial Structure, Financial development and other standard growth-determinants). To this end, the following relations are postulated:

$$g_{\_t} = \alpha_0 + \alpha_1 FS_{\_t} + \alpha_2 X + e_t \tag{3}$$

$$g_{\_t} = b_0 + b_1 FD_{\_t} + b_2 X + e_t \tag{4}$$

$$g_{\_t} = \theta_0 + \theta_1 FS_{\_t} + \theta_2 FD_{\_t} + \theta_3 X + e_t \tag{5}$$

Where; *FS*-financial structure (whether financial institution dominate the market or vice versa); higher value implies financial market-driven, and a lower value suggests banks/financial institutions-based.

FD: captures the overall financial development, encompassing development of banks, non-banks and securities market. Higher values implies deepened financial services.

X: Captures *standard growth determinants* serving as conditioning factors.

And $e_t$is the error term; whereas $\alpha_{s,} b_s$ *and* θ_s are the coefficients.

Key Predictions of the Model

Following Levine (2002) the following predictions are made:

- *Bank-based view* predicts that countries where financial institutions (e.g., banks) have dominance over the financial market (e.g., stock market), the $\alpha_1 < 0, b_1 > 0, \theta_1 < 0$ *and* θ_2>0; whereas

- *Market-based view predicts* that: $\alpha_1 > 0,\ b_1 > 0,\ \theta_1 > 0\ and\ \theta_2>0$; and
- *Financial services view* argues that efficient provision of financial services, either by financial institutions or markets, do influence economic growth positively and therefore predicts $\theta_1 > 0\ and\ \theta_2>0$. The results of the above equations are presented in the tables found in the next section.

RESULTS

Financial Inclusion, Development and Growth Model

Financial Depth and Growth: A deeper financial system is likely to contribute to increased financial inclusion through credit accessibility. Consistent with prior studies, we observe the impact of two indicators of financial depth on growth. Both financial markets and institutions' depths do influence economic growth positively. Financial institution depth, defined as domestic banks' credit to the private sector as a percentage of GDP, is a proxy for financial inclusion, while stock market capitalisation as a percentage of GDP measures financial market depth. The regression results are presented in Table 2 (&2a) below. These results indicate that a unit percentage point increase in private sector credit granted by the financial intermediaries leads to 0.0528 point increase in economic growth, measured as the log of per capital GDP. The result shows a robust positive significant relationship between economic growth and financial inclusion indicators.

The marginal impact of financial market depth on growth is positive but its statistical significance is boosted in a robust way by the inclusion of a national savings indicator in the model as shown in Table 2(a). The Ghana Stock Exchange (GSE) capitalisation ratio offers liquidity for private sector agents and it understandable why growth will be linked with stock market development. The liquidity it creates is expected to make investment less risky, resulting in economic growth as natural consequence. For developing economies it is anticipated that stock market development will have at least a positive, albeit weak, influence on growth. A non-parametric analysis of the indicators carried out using Spearman's rank (partial) correlation also revealed much deeper insights. As an example, the financial institution depth indicator (BC2PS) has a positive and significant relation with growth using the correlation at 5% significance level, consistent with the regression results in Table 2, market depth shows negative but non-significant impact on growth. The very weak negative results point to the potential for the use of the QR method as a robustness test, as relying on average-based models such as OLS and GLM alone could miss a significant relationship. Kernel density function as a non-parametric further check for robustness is carried out for all the variables. The distribution generally indicated that the quantile method is more appropriate (see Figure 2 ebove).

The computation of Spearman's rank correlation coefficient and subsequent significance testing is based on the assumption that the two variables are monotonically related. However, this condition does not seem to fit perfectly, as can be seen in Figure 2. The two variables exhibit positive, zero, and a predominantly negative relationship at various points (years), validating the use of the QR model that studies the relationship at a particular conditional quantile of the growth indicator. Since the computation is based on ranking from 1 (being lowest value) upwards, the MCAP variable and growth indicator (lnGDPpc) depicts weak negative average monotonicity, and hence weak negative coefficient of -0.1492. The significance test[6] result does not accept the null-hypothesis that both are independent.

Market Power can be captured using the Lerner Index (LI)[7], which is often engaged to estimate the extent of market power (Feinberg, 1980) and hence the level of competition that exists within the financial system (Jiménez, Lopez, & Saurina, 2013). Market Power is positively related to economic growth and statistically significant. Higher index indicates less competition and potentially lesser inclusion within the banking sector, suggesting a negative relationship with growth. However, the economic environment within developing countries with widespread market imperfection, structural constraints and institutional bottlenecks inhibit a competitive structure in the lending industry. These frictions could support a positive relationship between market power (LI) and growth. Onerous entry capital and other requirements for the banking sector creates market power as a necessary condition for the banks to remain profitable. The likely market structure existing within the banking sector often exhibits oligopolistic (when each bank is taken as a unit) to monopolistic-competition (when branch-networks are considered). This

[6] Number of obs = 23, Spearman's rho = -0.1492; Test of Ho: ln(GDPpc) and MCAP (%GDP) are independent, and Prob > |t| = 0.4968.

[7] Lerner index captures the vertical distance between price and marginal cost. It is therefore computed as the measure of the mark-up of price over marginal cost [i.e., (P-MC)/P].

form of market context exhibits market power crucial to stimulate competition for sector efficiency and ultimately, growth.

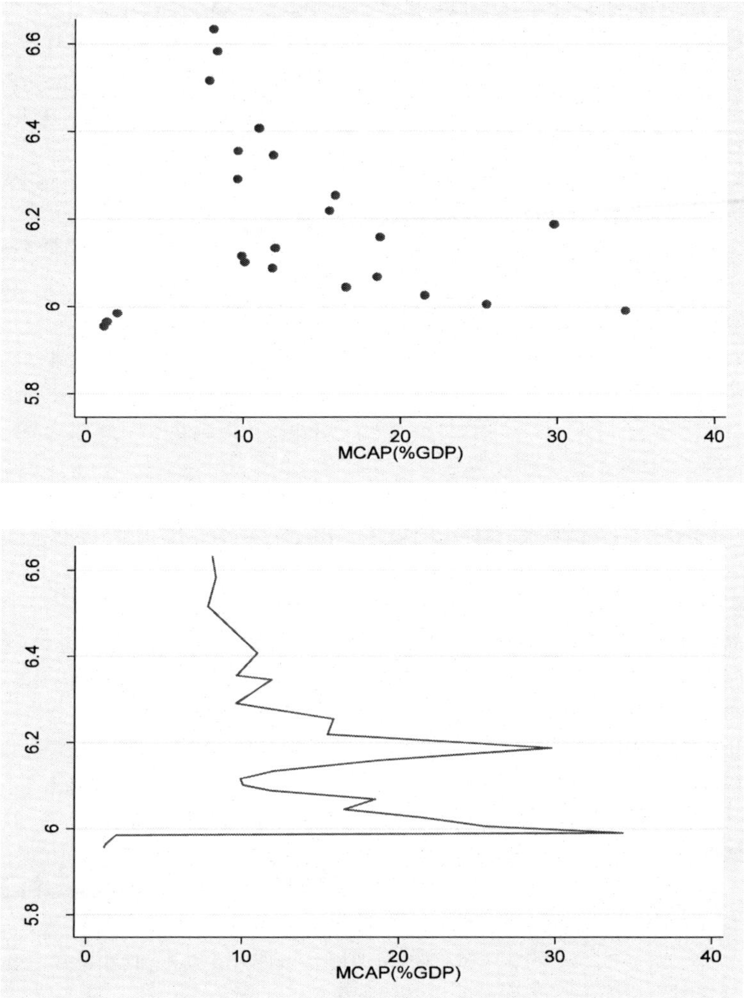

Figure 3. The graphical illustration of the monotonic relationship between economic growth and stock market capitalisation to GDP ratio in Ghana.

Financial System Efficiency and Economic Growth: The efficient operation of the financial sector that impacts on growth is a subject of interest in this study. The financial system's efficiency is observed twofold: market efficiency and institutional efficiency.

Captured by the Ghana Stock Exchange (GSE) turnover ratio, financial market efficiency is significant and positively related to economic growth (Table 2). The mean impact as captured by the GLM suggests that an improvement in the Ghana Stock Exchange (GSE) turnover ratio will significantly increase economic growth by approximately 0.02 percentage point by a multiplicative factor of the growth rate in the per capita GDP (i.e., ∂(GDPcp)/∂ (GSEt.o.r.) = 0.02*GDPpc). The quantile regression however produced varied results, capturing in particular the impact of the financial market turnover ratio at a specific range of growth. At the 90th percentile of growth indicator, the impact is negative, suggesting that the market efficiency reflects the underlying trend of the economic development process. The statistical significance fades as FDI and Savings are introduced into the models in Tables 1(b) and (c) respectively.

Banks' overhead cost as percentage of total assets are used as proxy measures of financial institutions' efficiency. Higher value represents less efficiency. Banks' overhead cost as percentage of total assets is negatively related to economic growth (see column II on Table 2). A unit percentage point reduction in the financial institution's overhead cost ratio is expected to increase growth by approx. 0.04 at the multiplicative of the average growth rate. The inverse relationship as captured by both the GLM and the QR models therefore predicts that banks' efficiency matters to economic growth. Thus, it impacts on the financial institution's ability to offer credit to the private sector at reasonable cost. The QR results however give mixed impact, as the model pays attention to each quantile of the growth indicator.

Inflation as a variable is found to be positively related to economic growth. The existence of excess productive capacity in most LICs means current growth and productivity lies below the full-employment output level. Given such economic reality, standard Keynesian theory predicts that growth rate must often be accompanied by a rise in the general price level, at least for the intermediate range of the aggregate supply. The empirical results suggest that Ghana's case is no different. Since the GLM did not produce significant results for this variable, it may suggest the average growth level is consistent with the Keynesian short-run range where change in price level may not significantly affect output levels. The quantile regression, which segregates the growth level along each quantile, could precisely determine the exact growth stage of the economy, such that the intermediate-run range could all be captured. Theoretically, it is only within the range where the aggregate supply curve slopes upward that prices rise with real output levels. Within this range, demand management policies are affective in affecting real growth but not without a rise in the price levels. Tables 2 (&2a) indicate a significant positive relationship between inflation and economic growth per capita levels throughout all quantiles. The median quantile outcome on Table 2 however, records a negative sign, though insignificant, maintaining that the variable is still positively related to growth statistically.

Table 2. Economic growth and financial development

(I) Ln(GDPpc)	(II) GLM	(III) $QR_{(05)}$	(IV) $QR^{\Upsilon}_{(med)}$	(V) $QR_{(75)}$
MCAP(%GDP)	0.00358	0.00322**	- 0.00400	0.00785**
	(0.54)	(3.78)	(- 0.21)	(3.33)
BC2PS	0.0522**	0.0222***	0.0177	0.0391**
	(2.07)	(6.96)	(0.22)	(4.36)
LI	0.983***	0.514***	0.712	0.254
	(2.84)	(11.63)	(0.63)	(1.88)
GSE T.O.R	0.0211	0.000737	- 0.00185	- 0.0371**
	(1.63)	(0.66)	(- 0.07)	(- 3.24)
Bank O.Cost	- 0.0432***	0.00792**	- 0.0265	- 0.00195
	(- 2.65)	(3.56)	(- 1.20)	(- 0.34)
Infla	0.00631	0.00262**	- 0.00113	0.00762**
	(1.03)	(3.34)	(-0.06)	(3.73)
U-rate	- 0.0420**	- 0.00907***	0.00575	- 0.0236**
	(- 2.49)	(- 6.36)	(0.11)	(- 2.96)
MoniGrowth	0.00718**	0.00383***	0.00209	0.00159
	(2.27)	(11.41)	(0.23)	(1.08)
REMIT2GDP	- 0.475	- 0.0752	0.153	- 0.346**
	(- 1.21)	(- 1.46)	(0.12)	(- 2.90)
NPA	0.0160***	0.00922***	0.00328	0.0191***
	(3.99)	(33.99)	(0.23)	(7.96)
LnFDI	0.00827	0.0742***	0.108	0.0917***
	(0.16)	(12.65)	(0.70)	(4.83)
_cons	5.270***	3.981***	3.663	3.797***
	(6.66)	(46.99)	(1.83)	(12.92)
N	16	16	16	16

T-statistics in parentheses * $p < .1$; ** $p < .05$; *** $p < .01$.

Table 2 (a). Economic growth and financial development (with National Savings)

(I) ln(GDPpc)-dv	(II) GLM	(III) QR_{05}	(IV) Q_{25}	(V) Med	(VI) $QR_{74.9}$
MCAP (%GDP)	0.00497**	0.00920***	0.00920***	0.00175	0.00155*
	(2.16)	*(177.65)*	*(21.66)*	*(1.48)*	*(2.87)*
BC2PS	0.0528***	0.0698***	0.0698***	0.0453***	0.0435***
	(7.73)	*(359.97)*	*(43.90)*	*(14.01)*	*(39.21)*
LI	0.499***	0.683***	0.683***	0.553***	0.560***
	(4.76)	*(202.13)*	*(24.65)*	*(12.58)*	*(21.93)*
GSE T.O.R	0.00414	0.000836**	0.000836	0.00811	0.00655*
	(0.52)	*(9.31)*	*(1.14)*	*(1.41)*	*(2.50)*
Bank O.Cost	0.00647	0.0138***	0.0138***	- 0.00759	- 0.00540
	(0.73)	*(62.63)*	*(7.64)*	*(- 1.23)*	*(- 2.31)*
Infla	0.00458**	0.00943***	0.00943***	0.00277**	0.00351***
	(2.20)	*(126.46)*	*(15.42)*	*(3.50)*	*(6.97)*
M2grwth	0.154***	0.197***	0.197***	0.153***	0.146***
	(5.08)	*(197.89)*	*(24.13)*	*(7.50)*	*(18.91)*
REMIT2GDP	- 0.497***	- 0.765***	- 0.765***	- 0.360**	- 0.329***
	(- 4.06)	*(- 236.60)*	*(- 28.85)*	*(- 5.15)*	*(- 15.19)*
NPA	0.00178	- 0.00311***	- 0.00311**	0.00290*	0.00265***
	(0.88)	*(- 33.10)*	*(- 4.04)*	*(3.00)*	*(10.99)*
LnFDI	0.0256	- 0.00698***	- 0.00698	0.0420*	0.0508***
	(1.47)	*(- 15.01)*	*(- 1.83)*	*(2.88)*	*(15.26)*
Urate	- 0.00411	- 0.00197***	- 0.00197	- 0.00776	- 0.00513***
	(- 0.70)	*(- 8.47)*	*(- 1.03)*	*(- 1.44)*	*(- 6.75)*
Sav2GDP	0.215***	0.248***	0.248***	0.212***	0.213***
	(9.61)	*(256.98)*	*(31.34)*	*(41.20)*	*(131.53)*
_cons	3.820***	3.964***	3.964***	3.686***	3.506***
	(15.77)	*(611.90)*	*(74.62)*	*(13.63)*	*(92.49)*
N	16		16	16	16

t- statistic in parentheses; *Legend:* * p< .1; ** p< .05; *** p< .01.

Consistent with Philip's curve prediction, we expect a trade-off between unemployment and economic growth (and inflation). The negative relationship between unemployment and economic growth is statistically significant across all the quantiles of the per capita GDP growth as depicted in Table 2 (&2a). However, it is only at quantiles 0.05 and 0.75 of the growth levels (Table 2 (&2a)) that unemployment rate produced significant impact on growth. The intuitive explanation is that rise in national productivity is often accompanied by reduced unemployment as jobs get created and the multiplying effect takes hold.

Monetary expansion in an economy operating below its long-run full-employment level of output is expected to lead to expansion in economic activities and hence growth rate of GDP. The assumption of existence of underutilised capacity, which mostly is the case for LICs, guarantees effectiveness in monetary policy, especially for a short-run period. Monetary growth rate is found to be positively and significantly associated with economic growth. Tables 2 and 2(a) show a significant and positive relationship between indicator of monetary growth and that of economic growth for all quantiles. However, the magnitude of the impact reduces at higher quantiles of the real per capita growth indicator. This suggests that monetary policy has a much stronger impact on the real sector in the short-run period relative to the long-run when monetary expansion often tends to be inflationary.

Domestic private remittance inflow is negatively related to economic growth of the receiving economy. Given that remittances represent income created abroad, its direct positive impact is realised mostly in the source economy where such factor incomes are created. Its contribution towards the receiving economy may be positive in some other respect but not towards growth. Stretching the argument further, remittances may create dependency for the recipients' economy as foreign aid does, resulting in negative impact on real per capita growth. This appears to be the case for the present study in which remittance is negatively associated with the real economic growth rate (indicator) in Ghana. The robust nature of the results across all quantiles sends a clear signal that remittance inflows may do more harm than good towards domestic growth and prosperity in the recipient country.

Gross savings (Sav2GDP) has a robust positive and significant relationship with economic growth. Consistent with an endogenous growth model, higher growth may result from higher savings, which translates into higher domestic private investments. Table 2(a) shows that savings level is significant across the entire spectrum of the quantiles for economic growth in Ghana.

The impact of non-performing assets (NPAs) on economic growth of Ghana is predominantly positive (from Table 2). Columns III and IV on Table 2(a) however reveal a negative impact per a priori expectation. Non-performing assets as a percentage of gross loans indicate a positive relationship with economic growth, which may appear to be inconsistent with both theory and practice. Notwithstanding this seemingly awkward relationship, a new understanding often missed by both researchers and practitioners may emerge.

As the economy expands and more financial resources are advanced to private agents, the reality of information asymmetry in the financial sector of LICs results in some loans becoming irrecoverable, and hence high default with the resultant non-performing assets (NPAs). In theory this is expected to have negative impact on the growth of the economy. The existence of NPAs affects the stability of the financial institutions concerned. However the credit advanced could find it way working in the real productive sector of the economy albeit their non-payments. In the short-run, loan non-payment does not necessarily have a negative effect on the growth of the national economy. It could be argued further that the non-performing loans may not significantly affect the operational efficiencies of the financial institutions concerned, to the extent that would jeopardise their ability to remain competitive in the lending industry. This explains in part, why, in spite of the NPAs recorded in their books, banks in Ghana are still able to give credit to the private sector, a situation which has led to more financial inclusivity. In the long-run however, the widespread NPAs in the banks' books lead to distress among the affected institutions, which ultimately hampers their ability to grant further credit to accentuate inclusivity and real sector growth. In these cases, NPAs could have negative impact on the stability of the financial intermediaries and ultimately the real growth of the national economy.

Log of Foreign Direct Investment (FDI) is introduced into the model to ascertain its marginal effect on growth. The linear model (GLM) suggests a positive relationship with growth, with no significant impact (Tables 2 and 2a)). FDI however has a negative impact at the lower quantiles of economic growth (q0.05 and q0.25) but a positive significant impact at the higher quantiles (*q≥ Medium quantile*) of the growth indicator (see Table 2-a). Given that the magnitude of the impact increases at higher quantiles of the growth rate of the economy, it stands to assume that the impact of foreign direct investments is realisable in LICs when the economy takes off in its developmental stage. In view of this, we submit further that foreign investments at the initial phase of the growth process may not be ideal for a developing country as infant industries get exposed to foreign competition that comes with sophisticated technology.

Given that FDI enters the equations, the study controls for the effect of global financial crisis on Ghana's real growth. Ghana's resilience in the face of the global financial crisis could not be coincidental. It began drilling oil in commercial quantities for the first time in 2010.

Ghana was among World Bank targeted lending beneficiary countries. This facility of the Bank aims at mitigating the dire impact of the global financial crisis, as private capital inflow was affected (Arieff, 2010). Besides, Ghana was among four (4) Sub-Saharan African countries benefited from special fund[8] provided by the US government aimed at reducing the impact of global financial crisis. It may not be surprising that the country though an LIC, is considered by IMF as one of the twelve (12) frontier economies in Sub-Saharan Africa.

FINANCIAL STRUCTURE, DEVELOPMENT AND ECONOMIC GROWTH-NEXUS

The structure of the financial system that exists in a country is key for determining whether financial deepening can foster inclusion and subsequently impacts the growth process of such economies. In keeping with the theoretic position that financial institutions (banks-based) tend to be the driving force of countries at the early stage of their economic development (Boyd and Smith, 1998), the composition of the financial structure of Ghana is examined to determine what drives growth. It is predicted that, as the country develops and income rises, more benefits may be derived from market-based system.

Table 3 (a and b) shows the regression result using financial structure (activity, size and efficiency) as well as financial development (activity, size and efficiency) as key independent variables of interest, with other standard growth determinants as conditioning factors.

The results neither support the bank-based nor market-based views in their entirety. However, given that most of the α_{1s} estimates are negative while the majority of the b_{1s}, are positive, suggests that financial institutions, relative to the stock market, drive inclusion and growth in Ghana. The financial institutions, compared with the market in Ghana, appear moderately efficient in promoting growth. Thus, the financial intermediaries (banks) are more efficient in influencing growth than the Ghana stock market (*see column II, b_{13} of Table 3-a*). In view of this, the financial structure estimates (Size and Efficiency variables) in the model confirm that the banking financial institutions are dominant in terms of *size and efficiency* compared with the financial market's (GSE) contribution towards growth. Financial structure *'activity'* however indicates that the financial market dominates institutions in

[8] Under the scheme known as "assistance for vulnerable populations in developing countries severely affected by the global financial crisis" a significant sum of $32.5 million was earmarked for Ghana.

respect of their relative impact on growth. Levine (2002) argues that it may not necessarily be the case that Ghana's capital market is bigger but rather, the institutions are not strong enough. The financial development model results (i.e., b_{1s}) also suggest that the financial (banking) institutions are still a dominant force relative to the financial market. Again, two-thirds of the parameter estimates of the Financial Development equation (4) confirm Financial Institutions (Banks) dominance as a driver of growth. Noticing that 'Size' is insignificant statistically leaves the Efficiency indicator as the only possible route for institutions to impact growth. In particular, the estimates (θ_{1s}) suggest that financial *activity and size* of the financial institutions are dominant forces in influencing economic growth compared to the financial market (GSE).

Table 3. Financial Structure and development on economic growth (with standard growth determinants)

(I) Independent Variables	(II) GLM	(III) GLM	(IV) GLM	(V) GLM
StrucAct.	- 0.0322(α_{11})		1.678**(θ_{11})	
	(- 0.33)		(2.36)	
StrucSIZE	0.542***(α_{12})		0.269*(θ_{12})	
	(3.23)		(1.86)	
StrucEffic	- 0.208***(α_{13})		- 1.853***(θ_{13})	
	(- 4.75)		(- 2.81)	
FinAct.		- 0.282***(b_{11})	1.745**(θ_{21})	
		(- 3.72)	(2.53)	
FinSize		0.192 (b_{12})	0.119**(θ_{22})	
		(1.60)	(1.98)	
FinEffic		0.238*** (b_{13})	- 1.722**(θ_{23})	
		(2.86)	(- 2.47)	
LERNERIndx	0.569***	0.615***	0.493***	0.231***
	(5.07)	(4.61)	(4.57)	(3.16)
Urate	- 0.0333***	- 0.0397***	- 0.0291***	- 0.00649
	(- 5.88)	(- 5.43)	(- 5.48)	(- 1.15)
M2toGDP	0.0759***	0.0532***	0.0501***	0.0269***
	(6.68)	(6.07)	(3.97)	(6.35)
LnFDI	0.0561***	0.0184	0.0289*	0.0584***
	(3.30)	(0.69)	(1.65)	(3.82)

(I) Independent Variables	(II) GLM	(III) GLM	(IV) GLM	(V) GLM
REMIt2GDP	- 1.346***	- 0.918***	- 0.957***	- 0.420***
	(- 5.02)	(- 3.47)	(- 3.76)	(- 3.79)
NPA	- 0.0233***	- 0.0138***	- 0.0172***	- 0.0101***
	(- 4.64)	(- 3.16)	(- 3.75)	(- 2.93)
Infla	0.0207***	0.0129***	0.0155***	0.00385**
	(4.39)	(3.41)	(3.63)	(2.18)
_cons	3.916***	5.485***	4.365***	0.143***
	(5.41)	(13.53)	(7.32)	(5.51)
Stats				
chi2	2284.9	1161.2	6898.3	
df	5	5	2	
N	16	16	16	16

t-statistic in parentheses * p< .1; ** p< .05; *** p< .01; Dependant Variable is Log of GDP per capita.

Table 3(a). Financial Structure and development on economic growth (without other standard growth determinants)

(I) Variable	(II) GLM	(III) qr_20	(IV) qr_50	(V) qr_80
StrucAct	2.7816***	2.1804*	1.8608***	3.679***
se	*(0.63484)*	*(1.1388*	*(0.01181)*	*(0.75273*
StrucEffic.	- 2.7023***	- 2.1257*	- 1.7627***	- 3.6328***
se	*(0.58059)*	*(1.1518)*	*(0.01174)*	*(0.73337)*
StrucSIZE	0.31653***	.26441**	.30783***	.33736***
se	*(0.07511)*	*(0.08688)*	*(0.001)*	*(.04788)*
FinAct	2.9061***	2.3793*	1.9668***	3.7272***
se	*(0.56227)*	*(1.169)*	*(0.01154)*	*(0.72409)*
FinEffic	- 3.0083***	- 2.4141*	- 2.1941***	- 3.8179***
se	*(0.58174)*	*(1.1462)*	*(0.01155)*	*(0.73557)*
FinSize	- 0.16367	- .02569	- .00403*	- .25168**
se	*(0.13751)*	*(0.15031)*	*(0.00192)*	*(0.07797)*
_cons	- .10356	- .71644	- .93188***	.64247*
se	*(0.5779)*	*(0.46864)*	*(0.00535)*	*(0.35042)*
N	16	16	16	16

Legend: * p < .1; ** p < .05; *** p < .01 b/se Dependant Variable is Ln (GDP per capita).

Controlling for financial indicators, column V of Table 3 highlights the growth-impact of the standard macroeconomic determinants. Regressed without the financial variables, the relationship remains significant and robust. This underscores the point that finance does not work to affect growth in a vacuum. It influences growth within the wider context of other macroeconomic and institutional frameworks existing within a particular country.

DISCUSSION OF FINDINGS

Financial Inclusion and Growth: Evidence from Ghana

The concept of financial inclusion is key if a deepened financial system will promote growth. In a specific case of credits that financial intermediaries grant to the private sector agents, inclusion ensures that viable investments which promotes economic growth do not suffer.

Using banks' credit to the private sector as a ratio to GDP as proxy, financial inclusion has a robust positive link with economic growth in Ghana. The use of financial institutions' credit advanced to the private sector offers a superior indicator compared with the likes of savings, account ownerships and frequency of instrument usage, as used by Allen, Demirgüç-Kunt, Klapper, and Martinez Peria (2012) as metrics for inclusion. The superiority of banks' private credit as an indicator of inclusion is informed by its direct relationship with growth. The use of account ownership, savings and frequency of financial instruments may be a misfit when attempting to understand the link between financial inclusion and economic growth; hence bank credit to the private sector undoubtedly translates directly into investment, production and growth.

The findings that growth results from financial development in LICs rather than from stock market development is consistent with prior studies. The significant contribution this paper makes is the identification of financial inclusion as a critical conduit that ensures financial development translates into economic growth. While prior studies only show a general link between growth and financial development (Beck & Levine, 2004; Levine, 2002, 2005; Levine & Zervos, 1998), the present study attributes such a positive relationship to the ability of the financial system to ensure inclusion as it develops. Growth in Ghana has been fostered by financial sector development (with bank private credit as indicator) due to its ability to engender inclusion in the financial system, as compared with stock market development.

Stock market development, as captured by ratio of market capitalization to GDP in Ghana, does not significantly influence growth in the same way financial (institution) development does. To Levine (2002), such a finding appears consistent with theory and other empirical works by, for example, Levine and Zervos (1998). It is argued that ability to trade the country's productive technologies easily tends to better influence resource allocation and growth rather than merely listing on the national stock market, which in itself does not ensure resource allocation. Consistent with prior studies [see e.g., (Arestis, Demetriades, & Luintel, 2001)], it is evident via this study that while stock market and financial institutions' (banking) development complement each other in explaining growth in Ghana, the dominant effect of banking sector development is significantly greater than stock market development.

The study outcome does not suggest non-relevance of the stock market in the development of the economy. In particular, given that it guarantees liquidity and mechanisms that enable economic agents to hedge and trade idiosyncratic risks, it makes a cogent case for the potential linkage between stock market development and economic growth. The issue has rather to do with the stage of economic development. The reality is that most LICs, like Ghana, have either weak or relatively infantile stock markets, compared with financial institutions and banks in particular.

Within the wider spectrum of indicators that potentially influence growth, it may be intellectually naïve to claim a direct causal relationship between financial sector activities and growth. This way, the role of finance could then be perceived as growth-enhancing, making room for other key determinants.

Among a myriad of standard growth determinants, FDI, monetary growth rates, bank competition measured with Lerner Index, and bank's non-performing assets (NPAs) ratio are all linked with the growth indicator. While FDI is positively associated with growth in Ghana, private remittance inflows have a negative effect on growth. The impact of remittance on growth of the recipient country has been mixed in most empirical studies. While this finding contradicts prior studies which often find a positive relationship (Mundaca, 2009), others either find no impact on growth (Barajas, Chami, Fullenkamp, Gapen, & Montiel, 2009), weak (Bettin, Lucchetti, & Zazzaro, 2012), or negative effects (Chami, Fullenkamp, & Jahjah, 2003).

Lerner Index captures the extent of market power that banks wield, and is positively and significantly associated with growth. This appears contradictory with classical microeconomic theory of efficiency resulting from zero market power as predicted by the perfect completion model. However, the recognition that significant entry conditions create huge barriers into the banking sector, is key to understanding why banks ought to wield market power in order to remain both competitive and efficient. The sector which typically reflects an oligopolistic market structure, where competition over both price and products ensures innovative services, ultimately enhances credit delivery and growth.

Of particular interest are the NPAs and their impact on the growth variable in Ghana. The quantile results on Table 2(a) throw more light on the relationship. At the lower quantiles (q0.05 and q0.25) of the growth indicator, NPAs are predicted to have negative impact on growth. The median and 75th percentile, however, gives a positive relationship. The implication is that at a higher growth phase of national economic development, NPAs may destabilise the granting institutions, but will result in higher output, especially if the loan is not paid but finds itself working in the real sector. The presence of information asymmetry, which often leads to both adverse selection and moral hazard, contributes to this phenomenon.

A booming economy usually ensures more credit being granted to the private sector. The possibility of adverse selection and moral hazard therefore ensure that as more loans are advanced during a high growth phase (higher quantiles), more non-performing assets result. However, as in the case of Ghana, the early 1980s recorded the biggest recession (low growth) and the highest NPAs, a development that led to the reforms in the financial sector in the late 1980s. Judging from this, it is plausible to assume that the economic downturn (lower quantiles), coupled with inhibiting financial sector policies such as directed lending, credit control and interest rate fixing, all might have contributed to the high NPAs. This partly explains the inverse relationship at the lower quantile of the growth indicator.

Driver of Financial Sector Impact on Growth: Institutions or Market?

In terms of activity and efficiency, the bank-based view seems to hold in the specific case of Ghana. The dominance of the banking institutions in driving growth is supported by the findings, except for size. This is consistent with prior studies, for instance Arestis et al. (2001) whose results support the view that financial institutions' (banks) development affects growth more strongly than the stock market may, even when admitting that both do promote economic growth. This is contrary to most cross-country studies on finance-growth linkage which often exaggerate the role of stock market on economic growth.

The financial system's efficiency in delivering credit for productive ends seems to be the significant channel through which finance impacts growth. For instance, two-thirds of the parameter estimates of the structure equation 3 (see results summary in Table 3-b) confirms financial institutions' (banks) dominance as a driver of growth. But given that the 'Structure ACTIVITY' is insignificant statistically leaves 'Structure Efficiency' as the channel through which banks influence growth. The efficient operation of the financial sector is predominantly driven by the financial intermediaries rather than the stock market. The efficient delivery of financial services by banks to the private agents in an information-opaque environment is key to ensuring growth. This may not be surprising given the infantile stage of the Ghana stock market relative to the financial institutions which date back to the pre-independence era. This, seen from the signs and significance of α_{13}, b_{13} and θ_{13}, though the unexpected sign on θ_{23} casts a little shadow, and hence weakens the impact.

The finding above is consistent with Levine's (2002) findings identifying Ghana with other countries such as Kenya and Egypt as bank-based using the 'efficiency' criteria; but attributing this to the inefficiency of the stock market is what appears problematic. Banks in Ghana have over the years developed more immunity and resistance against risk, allowing them to operate efficiently even in the face of an information-opaque and asymmetric environment. The explanations given above reflects the situation in Ghana better than the conjecture offered by Levine. Since both financial structure and financial development efficiency indicators point to the superiority of the banking financial institutions over the stock market, the outcome does not suggest coincidence (see Table 3-b). The results confirm De Gregorio and Guidotti (1995) earlier findings that the financial system's efficiency is the main vehicle of getting a growth-inducing effect of financial development realised.

In terms of both *size* and *activity*, the results suggest a complementary role of both institutions and markets as drivers of growth. This is consistent with the countervailing view that the impact of finance on growth should not be segregated into market-bank dichotomy, as both complement each other in driving growth. This is evidenced in Table 3 (b). This finding starkly contrasts with Levine's (2002) findings that classifies Ghana and other countries such as Jamaica and Zimbabwe as bank-based using the indicator of size measure of financial structure - *'structure-size.'* The argument that Ghana has an underdeveloped banking sector does not reflect the reality. This makes our complementarity argument a plausible case that paints an accurate picture of the structure of the financial system and how that contributes to the growth process. This position confirms prior studies which admit that both financial markets and institutions collectively influence growth positively (Beck & Levine, 2001, 2004; Levine & Zervos, 1998).

SUMMARY, POLICY IMPLICATION AND CONCLUSION

Summary

Since the pioneering contribution of Goldsmith in the 1960s in establishing means through which a country's financial structure could affect sector financial services delivery, research interest in the phenomenon has soared in recent times. Mostly taking the nature of cross-country studies, but paying particular attention to an in-depth-country analysis avoids the issue of overgeneralization and benefits from understanding unique country fundamental characteristics. This motivates the use of Ghana as a classical case contributing to the understanding of how an economy benefits from the growth-enhancing impact of financial development and inclusion, from the perspective of a lower income country (LIC).

Ghana provides a good case for understanding the relationship from an LIC's stand point in that it has evolved from various phases of financial systems, emerging out of the repressive regime in the period preceding the early 1980s, going through key sector reforms as part of the structural adjustment programme in the late 1980s. Prior to the establishment of Ghana's stock market (GSE) in the early 1990s, the financial landscape was dominated by banking financial intermediaries, some dating back to the pre-independence era. Against this background, it is only logical to expect that financial inclusion that facilitates growth is plausible via financial (institutions) development, other than the stock market.

Ghana's financial market is still at the infantile stage. But even then, its ability to affect growth through liquidity which allows lumpy and risky investment to be undertaken, cannot be ignored. In this sense, Ghana's economic growth is facilitated by the financial system as the institutions and the market complement each other, allowing for a deeper and highly inclusive sector.

Table 3 (b). Summary Matrix of the prediction key indicators in Table 3

Models	Activity	Size	Efficiency
Financial Structure [II]	- 0.0322(α_{11})	0.542***(α_{12})	- 0.208***(α_{13})
Financial Dev [III]	- 0.282***(b_{11})	0.192 (b_{12})	0.238***(b_{13})
Financial Structure and	1.678**(θ_{11})	0.269*(θ_{12})	- 1.853***(θ_{13})
Financial Dev. [IV]	1.745**(θ_{21})	0.119**(θ_{22})	- 1.722**(θ_{23})

Using a quantile regression model, and benchmarking it with a generalized linear regression model (model), the study has made a significant contribution towards understanding the role of financial development, inclusion and structure on economic growth of LICs, using Ghana as reference case.

It is evidenced from the study that for LICs, the banks' growth-facilitating role is much stronger than that of the financial market. This confirms earlier research that in higher income countries, stock markets tend to have more impact than the banks. That way, a policy pathway is determined; there is greater tendency for the financial systems of LICs to become more market-based as they become richer. But until then, the financial institutions (mainly banks) will drive growth in such countries as they engender financial inclusiveness across a wider spectrum of private economic agents through credit allocations. Policy efforts that strengthen the financial intermediaries in developing countries to enable them to ensure more inclusion become a promising conduit to achieving meaningful growth.

Policy Implications

The subject of financial inclusion has been a topmost priority for policy-makers both at national and international levels, as well as for donor agencies. Even more crucial is the issue of inclusion within the context of lower income economies where prevalence of structural bottlenecks, administrative lapses and policy gaps often tend to widen the exclusion gap. In light of the urgency of the issue of financial inclusion, the following policy recommendations promise to make impact:

1. The need to strengthen financial intermediaries to ensure much wider inclusion is a matter of necessity, if growth were to be realised in LICs.

2. Financial market development needs more policy and a participatory boost if the full benefits arising out of the complementary role it plays in delivering financial services in LICs were to be realisable.
3. For donor agencies, a clear signal is given: channel pro-growth funds through the financial intermediaries where financial inclusion will be a matter of course.
4. State actors and policy-makers aimed at promoting financial inclusion within the private sector agents can rely on the intermediary role of financial institutions.
5. To researchers and academics, the established relationship deserves further probing in other LICs outside the West African sub-region: financial deepening→financial inclusion→economic growth.

Understanding the relationship, as the study has highlighted, suggests that policies on growth, financial sector reforms and financial inclusion need not be implemented in isolation.

Conclusion

In order to understand the relevant relationship between financial development, inclusion and economic growth in an LIC, the study adopts an in-depth country-specific approach using Ghana as a case. This approach is a remarkable shift in the existing paradigm where findings of cross-country studies often fail to capture country-specific policies, structures, and the general financial environment within which a country develops. The recognition that the nature, operation and financial policies that are pursued in each country tend to significantly shape the mechanism through which the financial system enhances the growth process, motivates the focus on Ghana.

The study provides a strong case that the potential growth effect of financial institutions in LICs is much stronger relative to that of the financial market. Apparently so because while the former fosters financial inclusion as it deepens, the latter serves a different function that may not engender growth in the short-run. In Ghana's case, which may as well be the case for most LICs, the financial institution's establishment and operations predate that of the stock markets. In the light of this, inclusion ensures growth results from the financial institutions as they make credit accessible and at reasonable cost to the private sector agents. When this is complemented by the liquidity and risk hedging mechanisms that emerging stock markets offer, sustained growth is very likely in LICs.

Though this study does not establish causation in a grander sense, it makes a significant contribution to understanding the age-old finance-growth nexus. This it does by emphasizing the growth-facilitating role financial systems play in ensuring wider inclusion via credit allocation. As the sector deepens following series of reforms, inclusion becomes a natural consequence when financial institutions grant more credit to the private sector. This way, the financial sector enhances growth, ensuring that viable investments that translate into growth are undertaken at a reasonable cost. Growth therefore emerges, as the financial development reduce both transaction and information costs. This suggests to LICs the relevancy of the growth-facilitating role of finance which must be given policy attention to ensure sustained growth.

Direction for Further Work

The present study establishes causation within the limits of nonparametric analysis influenced by the small number of observations. In the future, researchers may be able to apply a Granger causality test for financial inclusion and growth. The operation of equity markets in LICs may be characterised as somewhere between a cosy club to money laundrettes. Efficient market testing of risk pricing in LIC exchanges is a necessary component for building an efficacious regulatory framework to support growth.

As further data sets become available, methods such as GMM may have much to offer.

Additionally, research on the subject focusing on other LICs is recommended. This will ensure that the findings in respect of the established causality in the present study are generalizable.

APPENDIX

Table A-1. Variable Definitions

Category	Variable Name	Variable Definitions	Source
Dependent Variable (DV) Indicator for Growth	ln(GDP)PC	Natural log of Real GDP per capita: GDP per capita is gross domestic product – (GDP in Constant 2005 USD) divided by midyear population. GDP measures the sum of gross value added by all resident producers in the economy plus often adjusted with taxes and subsidies.	World Development Indicators (WDI), World Bank
Financial Market Depth-IV[1] (regular indicator)	MCAP (%GDP)	Market capitalization as percentage of GDP: Total value of all listed shares in a stock market as a percentage of GDP[2].	Global Stock Markets Factbook and supplemental S&P data, Standard and Poor's (Reported by World Bank)
Financial Institutions Depth-Proxy for Financial Inclusion – IV (regular indicator)	BC2PS	Bank private credit to GDP (%): The financial resources provided to the private sector by domestic money banks as a share of GDP.	International Financial Statistics (IFS), International Monetary Fund (IMF)
Proxy for Banking sector competitive behaviour - IV (conditioning variable)	LI.	Lerner Index (LI): A measure of market power in the banking market. It compares output pricing and marginal costs (that is, mark-up). An increase in the Lerner index indicates reduced competitive conducts among financial intermediaries.	Bankscope, Bureau van Dijk (BvD) (Reported by World Bank)

[1] IV-denoting independent variable.

[2] The figures are deflated using the following methodology: $\{(0.5)*[Ft/P_{et} + F_{t-1}/P_{\_et-1}]\}/[GDPt/P_{at}]$ where F is stock market capitalization, P_e is end-of period CPI, and P_a is average annual CPI.

Category	Variable Name	Variable Definitions	Source
Stock Market Efficiency - IV (regular indicator)	GSET.O.R.	Stock market turnover ratio (%): Total value of shares traded during the period divided by the average market capitalization for the period.	Global Stock Markets Factbook and supplemental S&P data, Standard and Poor' (Reported by World Bank)
Measure of Financial Institution's Efficiency - IV (regular indicator)	Bank O. Cost	Bank overhead costs to total assets (%): Operating expenses of a bank as a share of the value of all assets held. Total assets include total earning assets, cash and due from banks, foreclosed real estate, fixed assets, goodwill, other intangibles, current tax assets, deferred tax assets, discontinued operations and other assets.	Bankscope, Bureau van Dijk (BvD) (Reported by World Bank)
Measure of impact of general Price Level IV (conditioning variable)	Infla	Inflation using consumer price index reflects the annual percentage change in the cost to the average consumer of acquiring a basket of goods and services that may be fixed or changed at specified intervals, such as yearly.	International Monetary Fund, International Financial Statistics and data files (Reported by World Bank)
Measure of Monetary expansion- IV (conditioning variable)	M2grwth	Money and quasi money growth (annual %): Average annual growth rate in money and quasi money. Money and quasi money (also called M2) comprise the sum of currency outside banks, demand deposits other than those of the central government, and the time, savings, and foreign currency deposits of resident sectors other than the central government.	International Monetary Fund, International Financial Statistics and data files, and World Bank and OECD GDP estimates (Reported by World Bank).
Factor income inflows towards private consumption - IV (conditioning variable)	REMT2GDP	Remittance inflows to GDP (%): Workers' remittances and compensation of employees comprise current transfers by migrant workers and wages and salaries earned by non-resident workers (composition: workers' remittances, compensation of employees, and migrants' transfers).	World Development Indicators (WDI), World Bank

Table A-1. (Continued).

Category	Variable Name	Variable Definitions	Source
Capturing financial institution's Stability: IV (regular indicator)	NPA	Provisions to non-performing Assets (%): Non-performing assets are loans for which the contractual payments are delinquent, usually defined as and NPL ratio[3].	Financial Soundness Indicators Database - International Monetary Fund (IMF) - (Reported by World Bank)
Productive international Inflows: IV (conditioning variable)	lnFDI	Natural long of FDI (net inflows): Foreign direct investment are the net inflows of investment to acquire a lasting management interest in an enterprise operating in an economy other than that of the investor. It is the sum of equity capital, reinvestment of earnings, other long-term capital, and short-term capital. This series shows inflows to Ghana from foreign investors, divided by GDP.	IMF, International Financial Statistics and Balance of Payments databases, World Bank, International Debt Statistics, - World Bank estimates (Reported by World Bank)
An independent variable used as conditioning factor	Urate	Unemployment Rate: Unemployment refers to the share of the labour force that is without work but available for and seeking employment. This is measure as the ratio of unemployed section of the active labour force divided by total labour force.	International Labour Organization, Key Indicators of the Labour Market database. (Reported by World Bank)
Proxy for national Savings - IV (conditioning variable)	Sav2GDP	Gross savings (% of GDP): Gross savings are calculated as gross national income less total consumption, plus net transfers.	World Bank national accounts data, and OECD National Accounts data files (Reported by World Bank)

[3] The ratio is determined as the value of nonperforming loans divided by the total value of the loan portfolio.

REFERENCES

Adu, G., Marbuah, G. and Mensah, J. T. (2013). Financial development and economic growth in Ghana: Does the measure of financial development matter? *Review of Development finance,* 3(4), 192-203.

Allen, F., Demirgüç-Kunt, A., Klapper, L. F. and Martinez Peria, M. S. (2012). The foundations of financial inclusion: Understanding ownership and use of formal accounts. *World Bank Policy Research Working Paper* (6290).

Ang, J. B. (2008). What are the mechanisms linking financial development and economic growth in Malaysia? *Economic Modelling*, 25(1), 38-53.

Arestis, P., Demetriades, P. O. and Luintel, K. B. (2001). Financial development and economic growth: the role of stock markets. *Journal of money, credit and banking*, 16-41.

Arieff, A. (2010). *Global Economic Crisis: Impact on Sub-Saharan Africa and Global Policy Responses*: DIANE Publishing.

Barajas, A., Chami, R., Fullenkamp, C., Gapen, M. and Montiel, P. J. (2009). Do workers' remittances promote economic growth? *IMF Working Papers*, 1-22.

Beck, T. and Demirguc-Kunt, A. (2006). Small and medium-size enterprises: Access to finance as a growth constraint. *Journal of Banking and Finance*, 30(11), 2931-2943.

Beck, T., Demirgüç-Kunt, A. and Maksimovic, V. (2005). Financial and legal constraints to growth: does firm size matter? *The Journal of Finance,* 60 (1), 137-177.

Beck, T. and Levine, R. (2001). *Stock markets, banks, and growth: correlation or causality?* (Vol. 2670): World Bank Publications.

Beck, T. and Levine, R. (2004). Stock markets, banks, and growth: Panel evidence. *Journal of Banking and Finance*, 28(3), 423-442.

Bencivenga, V. R. and Smith, B. D. (1991). Financial intermediation and endogenous growth. *The Review of Economic Studies*, 58(2), 195-209.

Bettin, G., Lucchetti, R. and Zazzaro, A. (2012). Financial development and remittances: Micro-econometric evidence. *Economics Letters*, 115(2), 184-186. doi: http://dx.doi.org/10.1016/j.econlet.2011.12.026.

Brownbridge, M. and Gockel, A. F. (1996). *The impact of financial sector policies on banking in Ghana*: Institute of Development Studies.

Cameron, A. C. and Trivedi, P. K. (2005). *Microeconometrics: methods and applications*: Cambridge University press.

Chakraborty, S. and Ray, T. (2006). Bank-based versus market-based financial systems: A growth-theoretic analysis. *Journal of Monetary Economics*, 53 (2), 329-350.

Chami, R., Fullenkamp, C. and Jahjah, S. (2003). Are immigrant remittance flows a source of capital for development? IMF Staff Papers Vol. 52, No. 1 [JEL D64, D82, F22] 1-48

De Gregorio, J. and Guidotti, P. E. (1995). Financial development and economic growth. *World Development*, 23(3), 433-448. doi: http://dx.doi.org/10.1016/0305-750X(94)00132-I.

Demirgüç-Kunt, A. (2006). Finance and economic development: Policy Choices for developing countries. *World Bank Policy Research Working Paper* (3955).

Demirgüç-Kunt, A. and Levine, R. (2008). Finance, financial sector policies, and long-run growth. *World Bank Policy Research Working Paper Series, Vol.*

Feinberg, R. M. (1980). The Lerner index, concentration, and the measurement of market power. *Southern Economic Journal*, 1180-1186.

Gockel, A. F. and Akoena, S. K. (2002). *Financial Intermediation for the Poor: Credit Demand by Micro Small and Medium Scale Enterprises in Ghana: a Further Assignment for Financial Sector Policy?*: ILO.

Gurley, J. G. and Shaw, E. S. (1955). Financial aspects of economic development. *The American Economic Review*, 515-538.

Jiménez, G., Lopez, J. A. and Saurina, J. (2013). How does competition affect bank risk-taking? *Journal of Financial Stability*, 9(2), 185-195.

Levine, R. (2002). Bank-based or market-based financial systems: which is better? *Journal of financial intermediation*, 11(4), 398-428.

Levine, R. (2005). Finance and growth: theory and evidence. *Handbook of economic growth*, 1, 865-934.

Levine, R. and Zervos, S. (1998). Stock markets, banks, and economic growth. *American economic review*, 537-558.

Love, I. (2003). Financial development and financing constraints: International evidence from the structural investment model. *Review of Financial studies*, 16(3), 765-791.

McKinnon, R. I. (1973). *Money and capital in economic development*: Brookings Institution Press.

Mundaca, B. G. (2009). Remittances, financial market development, and economic growth: the case of Latin America and the Caribbean. *Review of Development Economics*, 13(2), 288-303.

Pietrovito, F. (2009). Financial development and economic growth: A theoretical and empirical overview. *Available at SSRN 1439665*.

Robinson, J. (1952). The generalisation of the general theory. *The rate of interest and other essays*, 2, 1-76.

Schumpeter, J. A. (1934). *The theory of economic development: An inquiry into profits, capital, credit, interest, and the business cycle* (Vol. 55): Transaction publishers.

Wellalage, N. H. and Locke, S. (2014). The Capital Structure of Sri Lankan Companies: A Quantile Regression Analysis. *Journal of Asia-Pacific Business,* 15(3), 211-230. doi: 10.1080/10599231.2014.934627.

INDEX

A

B

C

D

E

F

G

H

I

J

K

L

M

N

O

P

T

U

V

W

Z